# A Diary of Miracles
# Part II

## Aliss Cresswell

Published by 55:11 Ltd

All Scripture quotations are taken from the New International Version © 1973, 1978, 1984 by International Bible Society.

ISBN: 978 0 9572642 1 2

First Edition

Printed in the USA.

This book is available from www.spiritlifestyle.org
or call: +44 (0)1244 630054
or email: info@spiritlifestyle.org

Also available from major online book sellers
and as a digital book download.

Published by 55:11 Ltd
email: distribution@5511.co.uk
for wholesale enquiries

# *Endorsements*

"A Diary of Miracles, Part II is the ongoing account of one of the most remarkable stories I know of. I have witnessed extraordinary miracles being wrought through the ministry of Aliss and Rob Cresswell in Chester, England. These miracles happen almost daily in the midst of normal life activities. This book is an example of Christianity as it was meant to be."

**Rick Joyner**

*Author, Founder & Senior Pastor,*
*MorningStar Ministries*

~

"Aliss is a normal Christian, normal as defined by the Bible. A miracle a day was normal for the first followers of Jesus. This book is your first step to being normal."

**Sid Roth**

*Founder and presenter of "It's Supernatural"*

"Once in a while someone comes along and decides to simply do what the gospel talks of doing; Aliss is the real deal. I've been into the shop and have felt the presence of God and Angels just waiting to deliver people off of the streets. These stories are true and real, a rare statement in these times."

**Kevin Prosch**
*Songwriter and Musician*

~

"Aliss' faith for modern day miracles is contagious. This book will encourage you to become one who will do the greater works. She and Rob are training up men and women ready to fulfill the Great Commission. They lay hands on the sick and see them recover; the lame walk, the deaf hear and the blind see!"

**Tom and Mary Anne Hardiman**
*Directors of MorningStar Fellowship of Ministries*

~

"Aliss and all her comrades at 'Spirit shop' in Chester are making the supernatural seem so natural, that it is becoming part of their everyday life. If every believer in the world followed their example in this book, I believe we would have the whole world saved in about 3 weeks."

**Leonard Jones,** *Worship Leader*

"Aliss Cresswell is a prototype of a new generation of healers and wonder workers who move in power in ordinary places. She is part of a new era of believers who understand the call of the Gospel to the margins of society, to the broken, the lost, and onto the streets. Her passion for people and her faith for healing is contagious. As you read these amazing supernatural stories, you will realise Jesus cares about you and everyone around you, and that miracles are only a heartbeat away."

**Justin Abraham**
*Founder, Company of Burning Hearts*

Also by author
Aliss Cresswell

## A Diary of Miracles Part I

## The Normal Supernatural Christian Life

 # Foreword

What surprised me most when we published Aliss' first book, 'A Diary of Miracles part I' was the tremendous amount of feedback we began to get from people who had read it. Messages came in that gushed with thanks and blessings for the encouragement and inspiration they had found in its pages. Many people told us of how it had spurred them on to take courage and step out in faith in their own lives. People seemed to devour it, relishing every last drop of the wonderful manifest presence of Jesus; often reading it through in just one or two sessions, telling us, "I couldn't put it down".

A well-meaning friend recently asked if the healings and miracles had stopped now that the café had been running for a few years. I think I knew what was meant by this, because it is true that as we built relationships with local people through the 'Café Life' ministry the focus inevitably shifted to more pastoral and discipleship work. But there is another deeper question here, 'Is this kind of supernatural phenomenon sustainable?'

'A Diary of Miracles part II' takes up the story where part one ends and almost as soon as 2010 began Aliss was pioneering yet another powerful ministry, but this time not in a residential community but in the commercial retail sector of the city. In a period of time when Christian bookshops were disappearing rapidly from our towns (unable to compete with the internet giants) Aliss stepped into the breach! However, she had a radically different approach, because traditionally 'Christian Bookshops' were there to serve the church community. Aliss' vision was to have an altogether different sort of Christian presence on the high street, a shop that would attract people from all walks of life into wonderful and unexpected encounters with the living God.

The message from this sequel is clear. The outward expression of any sustainable missional work needs to be relevant to its environment. In a residential community it may look like an 'eggs and bacon café' (like Café Life in Blacon) but in a town centre it could be 'a shabby chic gift shop serving cappuccinos' (like Spirit shop in Chester) – it really doesn't matter so long as the heart of the mission is to share the love and power of Jesus. Not only do ministries like this open up a well for those who come and receive but also for those who serve; because they also become training and equipping centres for those who are hungry to move in the Holy Spirit empowered life – this is what truly makes the supernatural life flow sustainable.

I hope this book inspires you to think creatively about the communities that are around you. Let the Holy Spirit inspire you to think big and step out of the box and into something new and wonderful and honouring to Jesus. Give God the opportunity to move through you to touch others in love and power and I guarantee you will not be disappointed.

**Rob Cresswell 2014**

A Diary of Miracles Part II

# Chapter One
## January

"Enlarge the place of your tent, stretch your tent curtains wide, do not hold back; lengthen your cords, strengthen your stakes."
Isaiah 54:2

*Empty retail unit, Chester*

# Wednesday 6 January

Happy New Year!! It's going to be wild. We had a lovely Christmas with my brother and his family who were over from America, where they now live. We enjoyed spending time with them, along with my parents.

I was back in Café Life today after the Christmas break and started to think about the teenagers who have come in and given their lives to Jesus. I began to pray for the teenagers by name and as I prayed for Levi, in he walked. He just came in to say "hi". He'd brought his friend Josh with him who grew up in Blacon but has now moved away. Levi asked if Jesus could heal Josh's deaf ear and of course we said "yes".

Josh told us his left ear was completely deaf. I put my hand on his ear and began to pray, "I take authority over this deafness and whatever is causing it. Any blockage we tell to go in the name of Jesus. Whatever is causing the deafness, I command it to leave now in Jesus' name. Lord would You pour out Your Spirit upon him and let him know Your presence, Jesus? Let him know Your healing power. I command that ear to open in the name of Jesus."

I asked him if he could feel anything happening and he said it felt as though it was 'bubbling'. He shook his head and repeatedly exclaimed, "That's pretty mad that is, that's mad!" He continued, "I'm not lying, I swear to God it's better!" He told us he could hear everything much louder but it wasn't completely healed so we prayed again until his ear opened completely. It only took a few minutes. We captured it all on video.

I told him that Jesus loves him very much and asked if he would like to know Jesus. He replied that he would, so we prayed with him and he invited Jesus to come into his life.

*Praying for Josh's ear*

Later, another teenager who often takes drugs came into the café. He explained that he wanted to get high on the Holy Spirit instead of his usual drugs. His friends had told him how they'd experienced the Holy Spirit in the café so he'd come in to find out what it was all about. We prayed with him and he described the wonderful feeling he now had of peace and love.

We told him that it's the presence of Jesus he could sense, and would he like to know Jesus personally? He did, so he prayed out and asked God to forgive him, he thanked Jesus for dying on the cross for him and he invited Him into his life. He was smiling.

Terry Fingers came into the café too. He's doing well and is still telling anyone who will listen how Jesus miraculously made the glass come out of his hands and his foot and how he has given his life to Jesus. He also shares how he saved someone's life after they were crossing the road in front of a car, and how he had stepped out with his Bible in his hand and pulled them to safety.

Blacon is deep in snow. It's so quiet, apart from youngsters throwing snowballs at each other and dogs barking.

*Café Life in the snow*

## Thursday 7 January

Rob is working in the café every Thursday now instead of me. He quite enjoys cooking so he's offered to cook every Thursday. It's such hard work trying to juggle bacon, sausages and eggs (well, maybe 'juggle' is the wrong word), but he seems to manage it. I'd rather be talking to the customers or working the till.

## Friday 8 January

It was -15 degrees Celsius (5 degrees Fahrenheit) last night! That's unusually cold for the UK.

A young woman in her early 20s came into the café today and stayed for about two hours. I hadn't met her before. She's had kidney stones and been in hospital so we prayed for her. She told us she'd read the Bible through five times, but still wasn't a Christian. I asked her if sometimes she seems to know things before they happen and she said, "Yes, it's quite weird". We chatted about Jesus and I invited her to give her life to Him, so she did. As we were praying she began to shake and before long she was baptised in the Holy Spirit as we read Acts chapter 2 together. We were both laughing so much as we felt waves of the Holy Spirit crashing over us and she said she was burning up like she was on fire. She explained that she'd never felt anything like this before; she was amazed and had never experienced such a feeling of happiness.

She looked healthy but I kept hearing the word 'anorexia' in my mind, so I asked her if she was suffering from that condition and she told me she was. We prayed together and she was freed from some evil spirits. Then she began to prophesy to me that I would reach millions of people with the good news about Jesus. She said she felt so much lighter than before.

Another young woman came into the café who had given her life to Jesus in there a couple of months ago. This time she brought her sister in with her and told us she was deaf in one ear. Apparently she'd had so many infections which had caused the bones to erode and she needed an operation: a hole would be made behind her ear and a hearing device inserted, which, of course, she wasn't looking forward to.

So I told her about Jesus and asked if she would prefer a miracle to an operation. She let me put my hand over her ear and I prayed in the name of Jesus. She looked surprised as her ear tingled and glowed with heat. In a matter of seconds she could hear her friend's whisper whereas before she could hear nothing through that ear at all. Jesus is wonderful.

## Saturday 9 January

Fifteen years ago today our daughter was stillborn when I was nine months pregnant. I'm so glad that she's with Jesus and we're going to see her again. It was amazing the way the Lord carried us through that time, I know I couldn't have done it without Him. We always remember her on this day and try to do something special as a family.

## Sunday 10 January

I love our church family. It was great to see two teenagers come to church this morning who had recently got saved in the café. They don't normally come; they call the café their church and they're not keen on getting up on a Sunday morning. We are rethinking the way we do 'church' now. In fact, most of the people who have recently chosen to follow Jesus do not attend any type of organised 'church' meeting. However, they come into the café regularly and we're able to teach them how to follow Jesus, both in small groups and individually.

## Monday 11 January

Rob and I spoke at another local ministry today on 'Hearing God's Voice', and then we went into a time of ministry which was great. We prophesied and shared some 'words of knowledge' with the people (things we couldn't naturally have known) and then we encouraged the congregation to have a go, which they did.

## Wednesday 13 January

More teenagers came into the café today asking to see the 'Jesus lady'. I think they meant me! They wanted to experience a touch from Jesus and to receive prophetic words, so we prayed with them and shared God's heart of love for them. Most of them have never known love before. Some of them have a parent in prison, or an alcoholic father or an addict for a mother and have been told they're not wanted and won't amount to anything. The kids who come into the café to talk to us have mostly dropped out of school at the age of 13 or 14. They often steal instead of working for money, and regularly smoke cannabis as they walk the streets and vandalise whatever they can out of boredom. But we love them and it's amazing to watch their countenance change as we share God's love with them and speak words of destiny and hope over them. Prophecy is so powerful.

A guy came into the café today and stayed for a long time. He said that I'd prayed for him briefly last week and he felt an intense heat and power and it freaked him out. He'd come back today but he felt that he was full of demons and was scared. I prayed again and he looked shocked. He explained that his soul, mind and body just connected for the first time ever, then he went on to describe how he had felt himself being pulled out of his body and was looking down on the café and finally descended back into his body. With eyes wide like saucers and in a strange demonic voice he said repeatedly, "You have the power of God, you have the power of God, you have the power of God." I replied, "Well, yeah I know."

# Thursday 14 January

We're planning to set up an online store to sell MorningStar products in Europe. We don't have an office or a church building, so I've been wondering where we're going to store all the books. I was imagining them sitting in our home and getting in the way. But since we now have a part time administrator, I'm wondering if we should rent an office somewhere and then we won't need to clutter up our home with boxes.

# Friday 15 January

Something is definitely happening in the Spirit realm. I'm sensing a breakthrough but I'm not exactly sure what it's going to look like. Feeling excited but I don't know why.

Two young guys came into the café today. One of them had recently given his life to Jesus at one of our 'School of the Spirit' meetings when he came in off the streets. Today he asked for prayer for his cold and wanted to be baptised in the Holy Spirit so we prayed for him and it was good. He told his friend that he should get saved too.

A family with four children drove a few hundred miles from South Wales just to visit our café. We prayed and prophesied over them. The café was busy today; there weren't enough seats for everyone to sit down. People were packed in. We were rushed off our feet but it was interesting to listen to customers' conversations. Some were chatting to their friends over their bacon and eggs, one or two were swapping prison stories, some were receiving prayer and others were sharing how they had been set free from demons!

A lady drove from North Wales with her thirteen year old son who apparently had grown too fast for his tendons. His knee was lumpy and painful. However, as soon as we prayed he was jumping up and down and laughing. All the pain had gone and his knee looked normal again.

Three local teenagers who are often in trouble with the Police came to our weekly 'School of the Spirit' meeting tonight. They were sitting on a bench in the lobby and we asked the Holy Spirit to come. One of them was so whacked by the Holy Spirit, he keeled over and no-one could rouse him; he looked unconscious. His friend was quite concerned about him, but he soon left his friend under the power of the Holy Spirit as he watched a large tumour in his other friend's arm shrink before his eyes as we told it to go in the name of Jesus.

## Saturday 16 January

We had a busy day off today, with pastoral issues that we needed to attend to, food donations and a family birthday party. Also, I've been considering renting an office, but I think I've had a brain wave! I'm beginning to wonder if we could open a Christian bookshop. The way I see it is that if we are going to have a load of books and CDs sitting around, and an administrator working in the same space, we may as well have the books for sale on the shelves. Perhaps our administrator, Margaret, could look after the shop whilst also doing the paperwork. I spoke to her about the idea and it turns out that she's always wanted to have a shop. It's just an idea, but it won't go away! There were a number of Christian bookshops in Chester but gradually they have all closed down and the last one will be closing in the next week or so. This is happening throughout the UK because of people buying on the internet. It's a shame but maybe we can do something about it.

## Sunday 17 January

Rob and I were invited to speak at a church in North Wales this morning, and afterwards we ministered to the congregation with words of knowledge, prophecy and healing. We encouraged the teenagers to get involved and it was wonderful to see them doing miracles and getting words of knowledge, some for the first time. A woman with back pain felt her hips move into place as the pain left and someone with a jaw problem was healed. Another woman who couldn't cross her legs whilst sitting down had her hips healed and she was able to cross her legs for the first time in years. It was a powerful time.

I chatted to Rob about the idea of renting a shop in the city of Chester. He said he has no space in his brain for anything like that, but he's happy for Margaret and me to go and have a look at some shop units! I've spotted two on the internet both on Northgate Street, one of the main streets in the centre of Chester. One of the words the Lord has continually given me over the past four years is Ezekiel 44:4, "The man brought me by way of the north gate to the front of the Temple. I looked and saw the glory of the Lord filling the Temple of the Lord and I fell face down." So Northgate Street seems to be a good location for us.

## Monday 18 January

Margaret and I went to view two shops on Northgate Street today - numbers 98 and 120. 120 seemed like a good number to me (as it was 120 who were praying in the Upper Room at Pentecost), but before we left home, I asked the Holy Spirit to make it clear which one, if either, we should rent. First of all we went to number 98 and both really liked it. It's a strange shape; long and narrow with a pillar in the centre, but the windows are deep set and there are also two rooms upstairs. It felt right. Then we went to number 120 but the agent couldn't get his key to turn in the lock. He struggled for about ten minutes and became very red in the face. He said he'd used the same key twenty times before, but for some reason it wouldn't turn today. I told him we'd asked the Lord to make it clear to us which shop to take, so there was probably an angel standing on the other side of the door preventing us from entering, at which point he gave a strange grunt and continued struggling with the key with his head down, but to no avail! We never did manage to get inside.

*The day we viewed the shop*

Since visiting 98 Northgate Street this morning, I'm even more excited. We could easily stock other books and CDs in the shop, not just those from MorningStar. And since we'll need shelves to display them on, I thought we could buy in stylish bookshelves and display cabinets that we put for sale as well. In fact, since one of my passions is interior design, we could also stock other pieces of furniture in the style that I like – 'shabby chic' and painted country furniture. I love French, English country and Scandinavian style interiors. Also, we could sell lovely gifts and jewellery too. And why not have some comfortable leather seating – sofas and tub chairs with coffee tables - a bit like Starbucks, selling fresh fair-trade coffee and cake? Wow! It would work really well in that shop. It's been empty for a year, partly due to the economic climate, but also because it's a strange shape, but that would work in our favour with different areas for coffee and gifts. My heart is to reach people with the love and power of God, and if we have plenty of beautiful things that would attract people into the shop, we could share Jesus with them, just as we do in our café in Blacon.

I spent the evening dreaming of a shop and deciding which MorningStar books we should stock.

## Tuesday 19 January

I only had two hours of sleep last night. I think I'm too excited to sleep and have been planning what we're going to do. Now I'm too tired to do anything. I had a chat with Rob who is happy for me to go ahead with the shop as long as he doesn't have to get involved. Then I called the agent and made a low offer of rent on the shop. Lord we need your favour! I heard that the last Christian bookshop in Chester will probably be closing this week.

## Wednesday 20 January

The agent contacted me and apparently the Landlord has turned down my offer, which doesn't surprise me. I only offered one third of the asking price so it was a bit cheeky! I increased my offer and am now waiting to hear. I do hope we get it. I can't see any other shops that look suitable or that we can afford.

Everyone who came into the Blacon café today seemed to be plagued by evil spirits. Anyway, either the demons left or the people left with their demons, but with the latter, I did explain how to be free from them if they would follow Jesus.

## Friday 22 January

Well, the Landlord is asking for more money, so I offered a bit more yesterday. But now I've heard that he's out of the country so hopefully I'll get a reply on Monday. All this excitement is wearing me out!

The café is amazing. What a glorious day. An 11 year old boy came in with his mum and he gave his life to Jesus. I prayed with his mum who has a heart condition and needs an operation. She didn't look well. A young guy came in for a take-out bacon sandwich. He said he doesn't believe in Jesus, but let me pray anyway. He felt the presence of God strongly and then the Lord gave me some words of knowledge for him which freaked him out a bit.

Last year a woman began manifesting demons in the café and shouting at me, then shouting at all the passers-by telling them not to go into the café. I hadn't responded at the time but later realised what it was. Today she was back in the café with her two grown up daughters. As she came in I said quietly under my breath, "I bind those demons in the name of Jesus. You cannot speak or manifest in here." She began to twitch oddly and looked like she was in pain the whole time she was in there.

Six young guys came in. One said I'd prayed for his foot outside the café a while ago and it got better. Another felt the Holy Spirit strongly as I was talking to them. A woman we'd prayed with some time ago came in and brought her sister who has M.E. and her mother who has angina and arthritis. We prayed with both of them and the woman who'd brought them in felt waves of the Holy Spirit and gave her life to Jesus. She sent me a text afterwards so say "thank you".

Someone who works locally brought a lady into the café whose twenty year old son died suddenly in October. It turned out to be a young guy I'd heard about from his cousin and whom I'd offered to go and raise him from the dead at the time. I've been praying for the family and for the mother even though I didn't know them and today I met the mother. She was obviously down cast and grieving deeply for her son.

Jen came in today to ask us to pray for her estranged daughter. We'd prayed for her in the café last July and the large lump in her arm shrank as we prayed. She just popped in to say "hello". She hadn't been able to touch her left arm for years due to the nerve pain in it, but since we prayed the pain has all gone and the lump is tiny. I asked Jen about her arm and she said it's a bit strange, but every so often her hand becomes a claw and she can't straighten it. I told her it sounded like a demon making it do that. So we sat her down and helped her get rid of a few demons. Her hand looked like a claw as we told them to leave but then it went back to normal.

She told me that a local guy had laid hands on her and imparted something to her once. I knew him; he was demonised at the time but has since given his life to Jesus in the café, and been delivered. So she asked God to forgive her for letting him do that and then I asked if she knew the names of the demons that were tormenting her. Since the guy had laid hands on her she said she could feel something sitting on her. It weighed her down and made her stoop. She felt it was heaviness (see Isaiah 61). She told demons of fear and heaviness to leave so they left. She made a sound like a train going through a tunnel each time the demon was leaving.

Thankfully it was time to clear up the café, so we were able to close the door, but a few people popped in whilst it was going on. Other demons were rage, anger, self-hatred and rejection. As well as the loud noises she was making as they left, she cried out with pain in her back and her arm. But then they were all gone. She said she felt full of the Holy Spirit - she was light, felt like she was floating and she was free. She began to laugh so we all joined in too. Thank you, Jesus. She says her life has changed since she saw an angel, got saved in the café and told us she now talks to the Holy Spirit instead of just to angels.

Our 'School of the Spirit' meeting was great tonight, as always. There was a strong presence of Jesus and the place was full. Tonight's topic was finding our purpose and destiny, which is crucial for everyone to know. I'm really excited about our new shop.

## Sunday 24 January

It was my friend's 40th birthday last night. We danced the night away! The church meeting was good this morning. We were invited out for lunch and then we went to the church in North Wales again this evening where we spoke on prophecy. The place was packed out. People were receiving and sharing visions and prophetic words, some for the first time. It was so encouraging. We stopped at the 'chippie' on the way home. My sister's baby is due but no sign of it yet.

## Monday 25 January

I heard that my offer on the shop has been turned down again. Well, you've got to try haven't you!? We're working hard and I'm quite tired, mainly due to the fact that I can't sleep because I'm so excited.

## Wednesday 27 January

My sister gave birth to her fourth child today. Baby Miriam is her first girl and my new niece and we're all delighted!

A couple I know came into the café today. I began to prophesy to them about a big heavy door closing behind them, like a safe. In the spirit realm I saw them push it shut, turn around and huge doors opened in front of them that they needed to walk through. I said it's going to be fun, I see a lot of glory and excitement and much fruit. They are going to sell and buy easily, and will be discipling people. I don't know what it is they are hoping to sell but I told them anyway and they made me write it down as they felt it would be significant. (Since writing this, the couple felt they should move from where they'd lived for a number of years and buy a house in Chester. It meant selling their homes in England and overseas to enable them to buy in Chester. Both homes sold within a few days in a difficult economic market where houses are not selling easily and they now live in Chester and are helping disciple new Christians!).

Michael came in today. He's the teenager who received the first miracle in the café when his broken ankle was healed the week we opened last year and later wielded the sword at School of the Spirit. Today he showed me that two of his fingers were broken. He asked Jesus to heal them, we prayed and they were healed immediately. The pain left and they moved back into place. He and his friend stayed in the café for hours, chatting.

Last week a lady visited from Liverpool. She'd told us she was suicidal so we'd prayed with her. Today she bounced in, smiling and telling us she'd been delivered from a spirit of trauma. Jen was back in saying how her life has changed remarkably since last Friday when she was delivered from a number of demons in the café. We'd also prayed for her estranged daughter and she informed us that she's heard from her for the first time in ages and she's coming home! We spent some time with a teenager who is being interviewed by the CID (Criminal Investigation Department).

## Friday 29 January

A young woman came into the café today whom I recognised. We'd prophesied to her a couple of years ago at our family craft day. We got chatting as she waited for her food to be cooked. She told me she'd had a bad car crash in November and was receiving physiotherapy for her back but she still couldn't bend and was in constant pain. We prayed, she felt heal and then bent over saying she was completely healed and couldn't believe it! She could even touch her toes. Her partner was standing next to her and he looked surprised at her healing. We began to prophesy to him about his job and he was taken aback at how accurate we were. I asked if they wanted to give their lives to Jesus, but they said, "No thanks, you're alright" and out they went.

One of our volunteers, John, was chatting to a guy and he gave his life to Jesus. Wonderful. One of our new Christians came in with her mum and she told me she had an abscess in a private place and couldn't sit down because of the pain. She'd had an operation to remove it but it had returned. It's an infected cyst. We prayed and the pain left. She went to the loo to check it out and it shrank, then disappeared and all the pain had gone. I prophesied to her mum while serving her food.

More people came in to share how their lives have changed since they've started coming into the café and how they've been healed and the problem hasn't returned. I love working in here. A teenager gave his life to Jesus and asked if he could be baptised. It was very busy today, with customers having to share tables.

The 'School of the Spirit' meeting was good tonight. I spoke on the Holy Spirit and there was a lot of joy. We had noticed when we arrived in the building that there was a bad smell, as if something had died somewhere (such as a bird in the roof cavity). The smell of death is awful. Also someone had squirted glue in the front door lock and the key wouldn't turn when we tried to enter the building to set up. After a lot of persistence we finally opened the door. I talked in the meeting about the Kingdom of Heaven and using your spiritual keys. I took authority and the key turned so we could lock up when we went home. It turned first time.

I had an email from Jonathan Helser and he's coming in September with his band. I also spoke to Nathan at MorningStar about doing a 'prophetic round table' next April in Chester. Exciting stuff. I should get a decision from the Landlord about the shop on Monday or Tuesday. It's going to be great.

## Sunday 31 January

I knew it was going to be a good day! Our church meeting was great. We had the 'bring and share' meal afterwards at our house, but the place was packed full of people, and children were going crazy on the stairs. I don't think we'll be able to do it at our house again, we need more space. We rented a church building so we could do some baptisms. We baptised seven new Christians. It was amazing. Jesus is wonderful. One of the people being baptised brought a friend with him and at the end he came up to me and asked if he could be baptised next time. When I asked if he knew Jesus he said he didn't, so I suggested he talk to Jesus which he did right there and asked Jesus into his life. We had trouble getting away, but then had to drive directly to the church in North Wales where we've been speaking for the past couple of weeks.

*Baptising Viv*

Tonight we spoke on healing and did it as a workshop, encouraging the congregation to share words of knowledge and pray for each other. There were many healings. A woman had one leg shorter than the other, so we sat her on a chair on the stage and put her feet on another chair, facing her sideways so people could watch. They witnessed the short leg grow out to match the other one. Other problems were healed such as headaches, infections, bad backs, necks, emotional problems, deliverance from demons etc. Wow. What a day. Tired but happy.

*Baptising Adrian*

(You can read about Adrian's dramatic story in Diary of Miracles part 1)

# Chapter Two
## February

"The man brought me by way of the north gate. I looked and saw the glory of the Lord filling the Temple of the Lord and I fell face down."
Ezekiel 44:4

*Northgate Bridge, Chester*

## Wednesday 3 February

I finally heard back from the Landlord about renting the shop unit in town and he's agreed to our last offer so it's all systems go!

## Thursday 4 February

We have a great relationship with other church leaders in Chester and we are part of 'Link Up', an organisation set up especially for the local churches to work together. Today I rang the leader who heads it up to let him know we're planning to open a shop in Chester. He told me that another organisation is taking over the last Christian bookshop that is closing in Chester and reopening under a different name. They had just called him yesterday to let him know. I don't think it will be a problem, but I don't want to compete with them for business. This new organisation from out of town wants to involve the local churches in the new bookshop. This may affect us, but I know the Holy Spirit is leading us to do this so we just need to go about it in the right way and honour the other business.

## Friday 5 February

I think I've been overdoing it. I rarely get ill but occasionally if I begin to notice cold symptoms I realise I haven't rested enough. My body is aching, I have a sore throat and I feel exhausted. Rob was being sick last night too. And he has toothache. We haven't slept much. It was just as well that the café was quiet today. Terry Fingers popped in. He's doing well. A young woman visited us from near London. She is running a youth café and heard about our café and has come up because she wants to see miracles in her place.

We prayed for a few people with various problems. One guy had been stabbed in the neck and it had severed the nerves to his arm. We prayed and he said his arm felt different and the feeling had returned. I was wondering what had happened to the young woman who'd given her life to Jesus a few weeks ago: I prayed for her and asked the Lord to send her in. Literally less than one minute later she came in and gave me her telephone number so I could keep in contact.

We had Godfrey Birtill leading worship tonight at 'School of the Spirit'. The place was packed out and rocking. Shaun who got saved last year was playing bass. One of our café volunteers wanted to have a go at getting more words of knowledge. He asked the Lord and he felt there would be someone in a green T-shirt who had a problem with their left wrist. He told me that he shared the word recently at his church and someone responded, he prayed for them and their wrist was healed. Then someone else in that church also responded. He was wearing a green top and he had a problem with both hands. He too was prayed for and felt the pain leave in the night, and he was healed. The café volunteer was sharing these testimonies in the meeting tonight when someone in the congregation, also wearing a green top had a problem with their left wrist. So they were prayed for and were healed too. Extraordinary!

*Godfrey Birtill at 'School of the Spirit'*

## Sunday 7 February

I'm still feeling rough and have now lost my voice. Rob is ill too but we're fighting it. But God is good. Lots of people are away but our church meeting was still pretty full. Rob brought a great message on seeing in the supernatural and opening our eyes in the spirit realm. Some people had visions which graphically illustrated what he brought.

A lady was visiting. Her husband was healed last year when the bone in his finger had snapped due to osteoporosis and he'd been instantly healed and gave his life to Jesus. His wife has a huge tumour on her back, like a football and also curvature of the spine. I couldn't let her walk out of the meeting like that, so we prayed and she said all the pain left. She was shocked, she could feel something happening. She was also completely blind in her right eye with glaucoma. She said it was black, she couldn't see any light out of it at all. So we rebuked the glaucoma blindness and told it to leave. Suddenly she could see her sister-in-law's white top, she described what I was wearing and could see people's silhouettes. Wow! We had spiritual and physical eyes opening today.

## Wednesday 10 February

I spoke to the owner of the shop today. We're getting the keys on Friday! I sent out an email asking if anyone would like to volunteer.

The café was very busy today. I spoke to the fire extinguisher rep who was healed last year in the café after falling from a great height 30 years ago. He said the pain which he'd had for decades never returned after we prayed for him. He has lots of questions about Jesus and wants to bring his wife to be healed.

Mandy who was transported supernaturally in her car last year in Wales was telling me how her life has changed around since that happened and she got saved. The work in here nowadays seems to be as much about looking after people and teaching them how to follow Jesus as it is reaching new people. We've had to change our concept of 'church'. Two of the teenagers who've got saved recently came in asking us to pray that they'd be given apprenticeships. They dropped out of school early and realised it would be a miracle if they got them. (I heard a while later that they were both given apprenticeships and are doing really well; they completed them and were given top grades).

### Thursday 11 February

Margaret and I visited a trade fair today in search of suppliers for our new shop. We had a wonderful time. It's so much fun! We were there on the last afternoon so we were able to buy a load of stuff from the exhibitors at knocked down prices but it meant carrying it all on the shuttle bus three times to the car park and then trying to wedge it all into my car. It was hilarious but we're very happy and having the time of our lives.

### Friday 12 February

We've got the keys to the shop! I'm so excited, but there is a lot of work to be done.

### Thursday 18 February

I spoke at an Aglow meeting this evening. There were

men as well as women there. After the meal I got up to speak, and I hadn't got far into my talk when a guy suddenly raised his hand and declared that he had just received revelation that he has authority over sickness. He said he had fallen arches in both feet and had to wear supports in his shoes. But he told us all that whilst I was speaking, as he received the revelation, he suddenly realised he was healed as he sat there. He was a bit embarrassed that he'd interrupted me, but was so pleased that he was healed, he was walking around the room and laughing. We all laughed too, and I asked if anyone else had something similar, so I got this guy to pray for the others too.

A woman who needed a new hip and was in a lot of pain was prayed for. She said the pain left and she was able to walk without stiffness. People with bad backs and shoulders were also healed. Quite a few responded to words of knowledge. There was a man who was scheduled for an operation on his hand in two weeks time. His finger was bent over and he couldn't straighten it; I think the tendons were pulled tight. We prayed and watched it straighten up and he could move it normally. He was amazed.

A woman came out for prayer who had polymyalgia. She said she'd had pain throughout her body for years. She told me her Pastor also had the same condition and she felt it was a curse. So we said a quick prayer and broke the curse off her and her Pastor and she was instantly healed. I gave a word of knowledge, 'brain child' and someone responded who'd had a tumour removed from their brain as a child but it had started to come back, so we prayed for her and she said she'd go back for tests to check it's gone.

## Friday 19 February

I spoke at our 'School of the Spirit' meeting tonight on past revivalists and the coming revival – holiness and power. At the end of the meeting as we were trying to pack away all the equipment and put the room back as we found it, a woman began to manifest some demons. We told them to leave and she fell forwards onto the floor. Someone had to rush and get a bucket as she began to retch. The demons came out and we were able to carry on packing away.

## Saturday 20 February

The woman with the demons from last night sent an email to say she is so much better today. She's been set free by Jesus and will never be the same again!

I've been too busy to write in my journal so now I'm trying to catch up. We've been working day and night; painting the shop, painting furniture, laying the floor, building a kitchen, putting lights in.

I had a day off today. It was the first day off in ages but I'm still planning what needs to be done. Rob walked up Moel Famau, a Welsh mountain nearby with some other guys from church. It was a year ago this week that we opened our café in Blacon. The time has gone so fast!

*Mens Walk - Moel Famau*
(Rob far left)

## Friday 26 February

This morning a guy came into the café. We got talking about Jesus and he told me that his brother is a born-again Christian but he himself is not a believer. He had a lot of questions and a number of issues. I asked him if he had any aches and pains. He told me he had them all over: shoulders, back, legs and more. He let me pray for him and was shocked as he realised all the pain had left his body. He experienced a tingling sensation that "felt good" all over his body and he began to smile. I answered his questions for him too.

He asked for a Bible which I gave him and then he wrote on the inside cover as I suggested he asks the Holy Spirit to speak to him as he's reading it and he didn't want to forget what I'd told him. He took some leaflets about Jesus too and said he would come to our church if he lived closer. He lives in Stoke on Trent.

Then Michael's brother came in. I hadn't met him before, but he let me pray and I invited the Holy Spirit to come. He began to sweat, but said it felt good, so did his friend. They both then said they felt high on the Holy Spirit and very hot!

A young workman from Liverpool came in for a take-away breakfast. He had a problem with his ankle, with pain every time he moved it and said he couldn't play footie (football). Most of the pain left when I prayed, so I prayed again and he said it was completely better. He was so shocked that he exclaimed, "Jesus Christ!" I replied, "Yeah, that's Him!" He kept saying thank you and went out smiling.

'School of the Spirit' was good tonight. The worship was great. Rob spoke on Nehemiah. Last Friday night we encouraged people to pray for each other for healing at the end of the meeting. I learned tonight that the people who had bad backs were healed on the spot.

### Sunday 28 February

It's been a good week. We're very busy still with

painting the shop, painting furniture, sourcing and buying stock. I've heard that some local Christians aren't too keen on us opening a shop in Chester. I'm not sure why.

*Rob & Ronke - painting the shop*

Our church meetings each week are going well. The café is still busy with many people being healed and giving their lives to Jesus, as well as the regulars coming in and doing well.

A couple in our church, Dean and Annette, want to be missionaries and so this morning a guy came from the missionary organisation they're hoping to sign up with. He'd asked to be the main speaker in church today so we agreed. It was amusing as he kept forgetting Annette's name and each time he referred to me he called me 'Pastor's wife'. He preached at us about evangelism and just assumed we don't get involved with reaching people with the good news of Jesus when actually it's the opposite. I couldn't keep a straight face, he really should have done his homework, but it was rather funny.

Sarah had a dream that Rob and I were catching huge fish in our garden and we had a large nut tree. I'm hoping the fish represent people who don't know Jesus, but does the tree analogy mean we're nuts!? Quite possibly.

# Chapter Three
# March

"Father, I want those you have given me to be with me where I am, and to see my glory, the glory you have given me because you loved me before the creation of the world."
John 17:24

*Our very first shop customers*

## Wednesday 3 March

Two workmen came into the café and when I began to talk to them about Jesus, they laughed and said they didn't believe in "any of those fairytales". But it turned out that the younger of the two had a bad pain in his leg muscle from playing football, so I told the pain to go in the name of Jesus and it did. Then I placed my hand on the older guy's shoulder and asked the Holy Spirit to come and He did. The workman smiled as he felt the wonderful presence of Jesus and wondered if it was a fairytale after all.

## Thursday 4 March

In Chester we are privileged to be part of an incredible group of churches across many denominations who work together, known as 'Link Up'. Each month there is a prayer breakfast for the church leaders. Often I have to work in the café so I'm unable to attend, but today I was able to go. The organisation that is reopening the other Christian bookshop in Chester was there, represented by a manager. I'm not sure where they are based, but they're not local. They presented their ideas and were asking the local churches to get involved and support them financially. It doesn't sound as though they have a workable business plan, but I didn't want to say anything negative as they are potentially a business competitor, so I kept quiet. They are planning to open in the city centre where the rents are extortionate and need hundreds of thousands of pounds from churches to make it work. I prayed a prayer of blessing on them though, as the more Christians in business the better.

## Friday 5 March

I'm aching so much from painting and working long hours in the shop, getting it ready to open. Rob is helping lay the floor, Adrian is doing the lighting, Noel is also laying the floor and fitting a kitchen. I worked out the layout for everything and bought the units, the floor, the work surfaces etc so I hope it all fits together OK. The place still looks a mess, but we had a large delivery of stock today. It's our first. I'm very excited, despite the aches and tiredness. I can't believe how much fun I'm having. Following Jesus is so rewarding. I love it. God is so good. I'm speaking at 'School of the Spirit' tonight on digging spiritual wells.

I just got in from the meeting. Whilst I was preaching, people were nodding off to sleep. I thought what I was saying was good, but they all looked bored and once or twice I was so close to stopping and saying, "Look, no-one is interested in what I'm saying, shall I give up so you can all go home!?" I had to try hard not to do that, so I kept going through my notes, as I felt the Holy Spirit wanted me to continue. I was amazed at the end when so many people came up and told me how powerful it was and how they had been inspired and touched during my message. It just goes to show you can't base anything on the way people look in church. Weird.

## Friday 12 March

Our friend Tim teaches at the Bible College of Wales – the one established by Rees Howells. He brought some students into the café with him today so they could see what goes on and they were asking lots of questions.

A young guy and his girlfriend came in. We prophesied and prayed over him. He's interested in knowing Jesus but said he wasn't ready, so we didn't push it. A lovely 82 year old lady came in, struggling with arthritis. I asked her if she knew Jesus and she said, "God yes", then said, "Oh, hee hee!" But she didn't really know Him and didn't know where she was going when she died. So she ended up giving her life to Jesus after we told her all that He had done for her.

A couple drove up to the café from South Wales. The wife has been diagnosed with ovarian cancer and they are desperate. They had heard about the healings in our café and so had driven all this way especially to be healed by Jesus.

Terry Fingers sat on the front row at 'School of the Spirit' tonight. We worshipped God with a drum circle and had a great evening.

## Saturday 13 March

It's been a good week, but I've been too busy to write. I wasn't in the café one day but I hear that Linda and Shelley were praying with people. Apparently a guy who had slept for three nights on his mother's grave went into the café. He had a problem with his neck and shoulder (well I guess you would if you'd slept in a graveyard for a few nights)! He was healed and then he gave his life to Jesus. He lives in Wales and had no money for bus fare, so the ladies gave him enough to get him home.

Sarah volunteered in the café on Wednesday. It hasn't been long since her son died, so she's doing really well to come in. She had a good conversation with someone and prayed with them. We have great volunteers. We took them all out for lunch on Monday to say "thank you" and to celebrate all that God is doing.

## Friday 19 March

My cousin and his friend came into the café today from the Midlands. I haven't seen him for years, but he wanted to visit as he'd heard about the miracles. He told me about an amazing vision he'd had last November of Jesus and how he'd dramatically given his life back to the Lord. It was wonderful to hear. After we'd chatted, we noticed two young guys having their lunch and as we began to talk to them, my cousin told them about Jesus and before we knew it they were praying and asking Jesus to come into their lives. We gave them Bibles and they were both so grateful.

The 82 year old lady who got saved last week was back in again today for more, as was Jen, who is planning to go to Sarah's group next week.

*Fitting out the shop*

## Sunday 21 March

We're hoping to open the shop next weekend. We've got 'shabby chic' furniture and gifts in the windows and already people are knocking on the door to see if we will sell it to them. It's amazing. We're still painting in there, and we don't have a till so I'm telling people if they have cash they can buy it. Many of them are dashing to the cash points to get money to buy the stock so I'm also pricing everything up too. It's a good start!

## Thursday 25 March

Rob was cooking in the café today. He said a couple who don't know Jesus had driven from Connahs Quay for healing. I think someone the guy works with told him to come to Blacon for healing. Apparently Rob prayed and he was healed. Also someone came from Colwyn Bay and told Linda that they'd been into the café for prayer a while ago and that Linda had prayed and they were healed the next day. It's wonderful to see others doing miracles too. It's the power of Jesus, available to all.

I love the way that my vision for the new shop is becoming a reality. It's very different from our 'eggs and bacon' café in Blacon. In the shop we have 'shabby chic' country furniture, beautiful gifts, jewellery, cards, Christian books and CD's as well as a comfy seating area where we will sell fresh, Fair Trade coffee and cake. When customers come into the shop they will have a wonderful experience of colour, the aroma of fresh coffee, worship music and of course the presence of Jesus.

We have sold so much stock from the new shop already, and we haven't even opened yet! It already looks quite bare. I'm going to have to order more.

## Friday 26 March

One of Shelley's brothers died, so she's been off work all week and it's been difficult trying to arrange for another cook to come in. I've been busy trying to get the shop ready too. It's all go! I'm looking forward to having a day off some time soon.

Justin Abraham was speaking at 'School of the Spirit' tonight. At first we thought he wasn't going to make it to the meeting! His car broke down as he was driving up from South Wales, but he arrived just in time to speak.

### Saturday 27 March

*Opening day*

Wow what a week! The shop opened today. We have named it 'Spirit' after the Holy Spirit. I asked Him if that was OK and He said that it was. We had an amazing first day. I love being behind the till, chatting to customers and taking their money. We sold so much; lots of books, CDs, coffee and interior gifts. We took more money in one day than I'd forecast for the whole of next month. I'll have to order a lot more stock. The main reason we are there is to reach people with the good news of Jesus and to demonstrate his love and power. And we did that. It was incredible.

A shop owner from a few doors away came in and I began to talk to her and prophesy. She told me that her sister had died two years ago and she still couldn't get over her death and was feeling very depressed. She asked Jesus to come into her life. Justin Abraham and his family had popped into the shop, so I suggested he give her some joy (since Justin seems to have an abundance of it). So he and his group prayed for her to receive joy which she did. Her teenage daughter and friend were there too, so we all held hands and they got blasted by the Holy Spirit. Also a lady came into the coffee area saying she had 'holes' in her eyes. She was in a lot of pain which subsided as we prayed and she told us she was pain free. Thank you, Jesus.

Tom from Ireland came into the shop and as he was standing next to the till, which is a fairly narrow space, Justin came over and began to pray for him. The next thing we knew, Tom was down on the floor, rolling around and guffawing. At the same time, two elderly ladies were browsing the gifts and looked slightly perplexed as they came across Tom on the floor. They looked across at me, so I said, "Don't mind the man on the floor, he's just full of the Holy Spirit", to which they replied, "OK", hitched up their skirts and proceeded to step over him, determined to continue shopping. It was hilarious. They took it all in their stride!

*'Don't mind the man on the floor!'*

## Monday 29 March

We had a good day in the shop again.

## Tuesday 30 March

I had a busy day in the café. One of the young guys I hadn't seen for a while came in and told me he'd been in prison. It was great to see him again. I gave him a hug and told him he's loved. He isn't saved yet, but the bones in his knee reconstructed when I prayed for him one time - He had told me his knee cap was smashed with a hammer and he couldn't put his foot to the floor because he was in so much pain. But Jesus healed him instantly. He wants a new life but he says he isn't ready to give up everything to follow Jesus. But I'm praying it happens soon. He was happy for me to pray for him which I did. He told me he felt light-headed and had a good feeling on the inside. I got a word of knowledge that he was worried about his mum, so I told him something from the Lord to encourage him.

He explained to me that the reason his life is so messed up is that when he was a young boy his step-Dad had tried to commit suicide by hanging himself in the garden. Not only this but he himself had discovered the seemingly lifeless body and been completely traumatised. I wanted to cry, but I hugged him and prayed with him for all the trauma to be removed from his life.

I'm praying a lot for these young people. It's time for real revival amongst them. I'm not sure what else to do.

Outside the café I saw a guy I know chatting to a young man on crutches, so I approached them and asked what had happened. The guy said his knee cap had popped out of place. It was swollen and painful and he couldn't bend it. I released some Holy Spirit power in the name of Jesus and instantly he could bend it without pain. Jesus, I love your power. Love you so much.

*Justin, Rachel and family*
*on our first day of opening*

# *Chapter Four*
# *April*

"For the kingdom of God is not a matter of talk, but of power." 1 Corinthians 4:20

*Healing ministry in Spirit shop*

## Friday 2 April

I'm sensing some weighty spiritual stuff going down. I'm not sure what it is though! Extremely tired too, but very happy. The shop has been open for a week now. We exceeded our sales targets each day. It was quiet today with it being 'Good Friday' but after we prayed for more customers to come, they came, and we surpassed our target again. Rona led a lady to Jesus and another woman came in who was into 'reiki' healing. She mentioned to my mother, who was volunteering, that the shop had a wonderful calm feeling. My mum told her it was the presence of Jesus that she could sense. Rona prayed with her too. I'm missing my daughter Romany who is in Florida for a couple of weeks, staying with my brother and his family.

I'd like to do some miracles tomorrow in the shop as I didn't do any today.

## Saturday 3 April

Well, I did a miracle! A family came into the shop and I ended up praying for all of them in turn. The mother had rheumatism in her big toe which she said was painful to walk on. As soon as I prayed, the pain left. I prayed for a guy who told me that sinusitis had kept him awake for 30 years! He told me his Dad had committed suicide when he was young. He felt something happening in his head as I prayed. I also prophesied over a young woman about her job and prayed for a woman who's interested in buying a sideboard. She was tearful as I was praying for her husband and daughter. There is favour on this shop. It's wonderful.

## Sunday 4 April

It's Easter Sunday today. We decided to have our church service outside the café in Blacon. It was great. Some people walking past decided to join in too. It was our niece's 18th birthday party this afternoon and it was fun going to see her and the rest of the family.

## Monday 5 April

It's a Bank holiday, so the staff and volunteers got a day off, but we wanted the shop to be open so Rob and I worked in there today. A musician from Liverpool came in and was telling us that a musical he'd written the score for is being aired this weekend on the radio. He was limping so I asked him what the trouble was. He told me that he had suffered from sciatica for years. The sciatic nerve in his leg was trapped and it caused him a lot of pain but the doctors were unable to remedy it. I told him about the power of Jesus. He explained that he was an atheist and didn't believe in God at all, but I told him that God believed in him all the same and convinced him to let me have a go at praying for him. I told him, "If there isn't a God, nothing will happen. But if there is a God, then give Him chance to prove Himself."

I was surprised that he let me pray for him, but I said a quick prayer and asked him, "Were you in pain before I prayed?" He told me that he was in a lot of pain. I asked him, "What is the pain like now?" and he replied that he could feel no pain, even when he bent over and did squats. He said that was unusual and he looked very surprised. His wife, who was standing behind him, said, "See! I told you there was a God." He was speechless!

A teenager who often comes to our 'School of the Spirit' meetings posted on Face Book today that she'd had a fall whilst ice skating last week and hurt her coccyx (tail bone). The pain wasn't subsiding, but apparently last night she had a dream in which I came and prayed for her and she woke up this morning completely healed. Wow! I don't even have to go and pray for people now, I can do it while I'm sleeping!

## Tuesday 6 April

We had a really good day in our Blacon café today. A woman who attends one of the local churches came in. She didn't know Jesus even though she's been going to church for a while. I got chatting to her and explained that I felt there was a spirit of fear preventing her from getting saved. She told me that another Christian had told her the same thing a few weeks ago, but she didn't believe her. However, this morning, she told God that if it was true, could He get someone else to tell her the same thing? Incredible!

So we had a chat and she said she did want to get saved, but then she was unable to speak. I explained to her that the spirit of fear was stopping her from speaking, so I said, "I bind the spirit of fear and prevent it from operating in Jesus' name. Let her speak." Instantly she was able to speak again, so I encouraged her to speak out and she renounced the spirit of fear and told it to go in the name of Jesus. It left as she coughed, along with some other demons, and she was able to give her life to Jesus! Her whole countenance changed and she was giggling.

I won a table and 8 chairs on 'ebay' that I'm going to paint for the shop. Happy.

## Wednesday 7 April

My tumble drier is back after being away for two months. Hallelujah! I sent it to be repaired after it stopped working and was told it would be back within a few days. After two months of calls and being told they didn't know where it was, it has finally arrived home. Unfortunately though, it's still broken. They weren't able to fix it, but at least they found it.

It's been a lovely warm day. I've been cleaning the house, spent a few hours ordering some stock for the shop online and then went to the Garden Centre for plants.

# Thursday 8 April

Amazing day (yet again)! I was in 'Spirit' shop today. I prophesied to a young couple covered in piercings and the Holy Spirit gave me some words of knowledge. I shared the supernatural knowledge with the couple – things I couldn't have known, since I had never met them before. They said it was all accurate and let me pray with them.

The neighbouring shop owner, Diana, who got saved on the day we opened came back in again, this time with her daughter and her daughter's boyfriend. She said, "Can you do the same thing to them that you did to me?" Standing in the centre of the shop with other customers browsing, I placed my hands on their shoulders and began to pray and prophesy over them. They were both in tears and visibly shaken as they learned of God's destiny for their lives, but it all seemed to make sense to them. I asked if they would like to know Jesus personally and they said they would, so they both talked to Jesus and asked Him to forgive their sins and come into their lives. They got rid of a few evil spirits at the same time and were almost glowing with radiance as the Holy Spirit filled them, and we had to hold them up to prevent them falling over.

Later in the day, just after we had closed and were tidying up, Diana came back and began tapping on the shop door, wanting to be let in. She had returned, this time with her son who looked to be in his early twenties. I let them in and they stood just in front of the doors, in the centre of the shop. I asked if I could pray for the young man and he agreed, somewhat reluctantly. It was obvious that his mother had insisted upon his coming. I placed my hand on his shoulder and said, "God, show him you're real." Instantly about ten copies of 'You May All Prophesy', a book by Steve Thompson flew off one of the bookshelves and landed at his feet. He was shocked! Mind you, so was I. I thought perhaps this was also the Lord showing me that this young guy had a gift of prophecy, so 1 enquired, "Do you sometimes know things about the future that you could not naturally know?" He nodded. So I told him that God had given him the gift of prophecy and I explained what that meant. I then began to prophesy to him and he asked if he could give his life to Jesus. He told me he felt 'tingly'. Thank you, Jesus. That was amazing.

## Friday 9 April

I was in the shop this morning with Roy, one of our volunteers. A woman came in and was browsing the gifts. We got chatting and she told us that she works in the local telecoms store but that she couldn't speak properly. She'd suffered from severe sinusitis for a long time and the doctors had told her they could do no more for her. Her nasal cavities were so blocked that it was difficult to understand what she was saying. She'd tried everything. We told her that Jesus would heal her and that He loves her. She let us pray and suddenly found she could breathe through both nostrils easily for the first time! She made her purchases and said she would bring all her friends in. She was astounded. She told us that she knows Jesus personally.

Some of the local office staff stand outside our shop and smoke cigarettes. Unfortunately the smoke blows straight into our shop and it stinks! They were there again today so I went outside and politely explained this to them. We got chatting about Jesus and miracles, and one of the women asked if I could pray for her to stop miscarrying in pregnancy. So I did and she was so thankful. Maybe I should have prayed for them to stop smoking too!

## Saturday 10 April

I'm tired but very happy. I was working in 'Spirit' shop again today and we were busy all day. A woman shuffled in, bent over her walker. She found it difficult to speak. I recognised it to be a spirit of infirmity and fear and as we began to talk about Jesus, I prayed with her and she was delivered of some demons and then gave her life to Jesus. She looked so happy. She told me she had osteoporosis of the spine and her ankles were very swollen. She sat down, we prayed for her ankles and watched the swelling shrink before our eyes! We prayed for her spine and when I told her to jump up out of her seat she did just that. She walked quickly across the shop floor, standing up straight - amazing. She bought a Bible and wants to start attending one of our mentoring groups. Thank you, Jesus. You are wonderful!

## Sunday 11 April

Something happened at the church meeting this morning. I'm not quite sure what, but Jesus came! There was such a strong presence of the Lord it was wonderful.

Rob and I were invited to speak at a local Brethren church this evening and we taught on prophecy and healing. We all watched as a ganglion shrank on someone's hand, a lady with a broken ankle said the bones moved and she was able to walk better, a back was healed, abdomen pain disappeared, a guy with clots in the arteries in his legs could feel them tingling and Jesus did other miracles too. We helped people get free of some demons. All in all it was a good day.

## Monday 12 April

We are very busy preparing for the MorningStar European prophetic roundtable. Unusually, everyone, including me, seemed to be hassled today, so during dinner this evening, we took communion as a family and told any spirit of hassle to leave (never heard of that one before) and then everything calmed down.

## Wednesday 14 April

We met Jim and Peg McLaughlin, wonderful Pastors of a MorningStar Fellowship Church in New York State who have flown over from the USA especially for our roundtable event. They like to arrive early when they travel so this meant we were able to spend a lovely evening getting to know them before the others arrive tomorrow. Tom Hardiman and Nathan Scott from MorningStar fly in first thing, as well as a load of MorningStar University students. We're excited about the Prophetic Roundtable which starts tomorrow.

## Thursday 15 April

What a crazy day! Rob was just about to leave for Manchester airport early this morning to pick up our guests, when the phone rang. It was Jim who we met last night. He said, "A volcano has erupted in Iceland and all flights have been cancelled in the UK." Rob thought he was joking and laughed. But at the same time, I was online and read it for myself. I looked at the airport website and saw every flight cancelled. The prophetic roundtable starts today. Well, we guessed there may be some spiritual opposition but this is ridiculous! I've never heard of anything like this happening before. How can they cancel every flight into and out of the country just because of a volcano erupting in Iceland!?

Those poor Americans - I'm not sure if they'll ever make it. I don't even know where they are. Their flights must have been almost to the UK when they were told to land in another country.

*Jim preaching*

Anyway the roundtable went ahead. Tom should have been overseeing it, but as Jim and Peg arrived a day earlier and Jim has been involved in many roundtables, he was able to head it up. Just as well, as we've never been to a prophetic roundtable before, let alone hosted one! Tom was supposed to be preaching tonight, but as they still haven't arrived, we asked Jim to speak. He said his church had prayed for them before they travelled and someone had said, "Lord, give Jim the word" to which Jim thought, "Why would I need a word from the Lord, I won't be preaching?" But God knew otherwise. He gave a great message and he'd even packed his favourite shirt but thought he wouldn't be likely to wear it. Many people brought prophetic words and were ministered to. It's been a good day.

## Friday 16 April

Tom, Nathan and Angie arrived today. They told us their plane was diverted to Munich, Germany. They managed to get a flight from Munich to Paris, they rented one of the few cars available and drove to Calais on the north coast of France. They spent the night on the floor of the railway station but didn't manage to get any sleep. The ferries were packed and long queues of people were trying to board and fill the remaining spaces. However, the three of them were able to get onto the ferry this morning and then took a number of trains from Dover via London and eventually arrived in Chester this afternoon. On top of all that, they've also lost their luggage at one of the airports. Wow, they are overcomers!

## Saturday 17 April

We went out for dinner with some of our American guests and had a lovely evening until we were walking back to the hotel. Peg tripped over a road work sign and landed hard with her chin on the tarmac. She split her chin open and damaged her knee so she was unable to walk properly. We managed to get her back to the hotel to survey the damage. We prayed for her knee and instantly she felt it was healed. The wound to her chin was too deep to be left, so we took her to the hospital where they fixed it back together. She was so brave. They inspected her knee and told her there was no damage, just bruising. I'm sure that was a miracle!

*UK 2010 Roundtable*

## Tuesday 20 April

The roundtable was tiring but so good. UK airspace is still closed, and many of our US visitors are still trying to get home. We took Tom, Nathan and some of the students to the Blacon café today. Adrian shared how he had been a psychic medium and tarot card reader for years until he gave his life to Jesus in our café a few months ago. They also met Viv who shared how I'd got supernatural knowledge from the Holy Spirit about her having a poltergeist in her home and how she'd given her life to Jesus and instantly the poltergeist had gone and her life had turned around.

We prayed and prophesied to a couple of sisters. One had a thyroid problem and her neck went hot as she was prayed for, without anyone even touching it. A guy they were with began to make a nuisance of himself and was talking loudly and trying to interrupt as the students were ministering to the sisters. I realised it was a demon manifesting, so I told the spirits to be quiet, in the name of Jesus. Immediately he said, "You can't do that!" but I retorted, "Too late, I just did." He was quiet after that.

## Wednesday 21 April

Carl, one of the MorningStar interns prayed with Phyllis today in the café. She had arthritic fingers and was barely able to move them, until after Jesus touched her and she was able to move them freely, without pain.

## Thursday 22 April

Tom and Nathan were staying at our house but they've gone to visit another church in the UK now.

Before I took them to the railway station, we popped into the Blacon café. We prophesied to one of the young guys. Another man in there said he had a problem with his knee and was in constant pain. The guy we'd just prophesied to, told the one with the knee problem how he had hopped in last year after someone had smashed his knee cap with a hammer and Jesus had healed it instantly. So we ended up praying for the man with the bad knee and he said it tingled and then the pain left. As we walked to the car, Terry Fingers introduced us to a friend of his who had just come out of hospital. He had a tube coming out of his lung and into a supermarket carrier bag. I'm not sure what was wrong with him, but as we prayed he said he could feel something happening and then he gave his life to Jesus. We had to dash as Tom and Nathan had a train to catch.

It's been a great week, but I could do with a rest. The weather has been warm and sunny; unusual for this time of year.

## Friday 23 April

I received an email from someone claiming to be Kevin Prosch, the well known worship leader. He said he would like to come and minister at our church. I can't believe it's the real Kevin Prosch, it must be one of our friends trying to wind us up. Why would Kevin Prosch want to come to Blacon to our little meeting in the middle of a housing estate? Anyway, I managed to find the real Kevin Prosch on Face Book and sent him a message asking if he had emailed me. He said yes, he would like to come to Blacon! My life gets more and more bizarre each day.

I worked in the Blacon café this morning and then dashed the two miles to 'Spirit' shop to work there this afternoon. A guy who had been healed in the café last year of pleurisy came in with his dog. Actually, I told him he couldn't bring it in, but he asked if Jesus healed animals. One of our friends was in the shop at the time with her five year old daughter. I asked the little girl if she would like to pray for the dog. It was only able to walk on three legs, I'm not sure what was wrong but it was obviously in pain. The little girl reached down and prayed for its leg. Instantly the dog was healed; it was walking normally and seemed much happier. In a matter of fact way, she was telling customers, "I healed the dog."

## Saturday 24 April

Shelley and Billy got married today! Rob did a great job at the ceremony. Shelley's brother was there – his broken little finger was healed in the café last year and his wife's blind eye began to see. At the wedding reception, we got chatting to his teenage sons about Jesus. Both had scoliosis (curvature of the spine). We stood behind them and could see their backs were crooked. As we began to command their spines to straighten in the name of Jesus, they started giggling as they felt a tingling sensation go down their spines and their backs came into alignment. They wanted to know more about Jesus so we told them and they both gave their lives to Him. One of them then prayed for his Dad's deaf ear. What a wonderful wedding. We had a great day!

*Shelley and Billy's Wedding*

# Chapter Five

## May

"Heal the sick who are there and tell them,
'The kingdom of God has come near to you.'"
Luke 10:9

*Spirit shop*

# Wednesday 5 May

Everything seems to be going well. Working hard but loving it. I was cooking in the Blacon café today because Shelley is on her honeymoon. I don't know how she cooks like this for so many people. I find it difficult getting the bacon and sausages and eggs all done at the same time and trying to remember orders. I'm only doing it because there's no-one else available. It was one of our busiest days today too. Typical! As well as cooking, I managed to pray with some people. A guy came in for food and had pain in his upper back. He told me it had been there for ages and always hurt. I prayed and he felt it go warm and begin to tingle. The pain left. I took some video of him telling what had happened and he showed me a huge tattoo on his leg of Jesus. He's a friend of Terry Fingers.

Also, Shelley's nephews who got saved at her wedding last week came in to visit. They told me they have had no pain from the scoliosis since we prayed. A guy from a local church came in crying. He explained that I'd prayed for him and his wife a couple of months ago for fruitfulness, without knowing they had been trying for a baby for a long time. Apparently she'd become pregnant almost straight away but now a scan had shown the baby to be small and dying. I prayed with him and arranged to visit them at home as we'll be passing the end of their road tomorrow night.

# Friday 7 May

I was working in the Blacon café this morning. It was really busy again. Deirdre who works at the Furniture Project came in on crutches. She'd broken her big toe. We prayed and she looked surprised as the pain went and she could bend it without any problem. Then a young guy called Martin came in for a cuppa. I was chatting to someone else but then we started talking to him. I saw what looked like a bright light on his face so I asked the Holy Spirit what it signified and realised it was time for him to know Jesus so I asked him if he wanted to give his life to Jesus and he said, "Yes". So he got saved and said he felt different on the inside. He had to go but came back again later to talk some more about Jesus and what it means to follow Him.

At closing time I quickly locked up, dashed home to get changed out of my café gear and then decided to get the bus to 'Spirit' shop as it's a mile and a half from my house and I didn't have time to walk. Often I wait a long time before a bus comes, so I asked the Lord to help me get a bus easily and quickly. As I sat in my porch putting my shoes on I noticed a bus waiting at the bus stop opposite. I locked the door, walked down our long drive and then crossed the road and it stayed there the whole time. I've never seen a bus wait there before. It waited for me to get on before it left. I worked in the shop for a couple of hours, then went to the bus station where I normally wait a while before the bus arrives. But I didn't have to wait for a bus like I usually do, I just got straight on at the bus station and noticed I was the only person on the bus. It's always full of people! As soon as I got on it drove off with only me on it the whole way. The only time it stopped was when it pulled up outside my house! Wow! That's amazing. Friday rush hour is one of the busiest times. God answered my prayer.

I was tired after working in the Blacon café most of the day and half hoped that 'Spirit' shop would be quiet and I could sit down. But it was very busy. I prayed with a lady who had been involved in a car accident last year. She said a cement mixer rear ended the car she was in. Since then she'd suffered problems with her head, neck and shoulder and she couldn't smile on one side of her face. I don't know if that was the muscles or nerves. The other thing was that she couldn't touch her nose with her finger (she would always miss) and her arm was painful every time she moved it. She's been told she can't drive. She said she knew Jesus and had received prayer a few times from other people but was no better. We prayed with her and suggested she choose to forgive the driver of the cement mixer. Instantly she was healed. She smiled a perfect smile, the pain left and she was able to touch her nose. Her friends who had come in with her were thrilled too. If you hold a grudge against people and don't forgive them for what they've done to you, often this can prevent you receiving healing or freedom from evil spirits.

Two ladies walking past the shop stopped and looked at the lovely window displays. I leaned outside and mentioned that we also do miracles. One of them asked, "How much?" I told her they're free. She came inside and took me round the corner in the coffee area and said she needed a miracle for depression and anxieties. I suggested to her that it may be evil spirits causing the problems. She didn't know Jesus so I explained that I could tell them to leave, but if she wasn't following Jesus, then the evil spirits could come back and bring their 'mates' and she would be worse off than before (see Matthew 12:43-45). So I asked her what she wanted to do.

She said, "I want to give my life to Jesus and follow Him. Please help me." So I led her in a prayer where she first renounced the evil spirits and asked God to forgive her for her sin and for giving these spirits a place in her life. She then told the demons to leave in the name of Jesus, breathed in the Holy Spirit and breathed out the evil spirits. She continued by asking Jesus to come into her life and I prayed for her to be filled with the Holy Spirit. She looked like a different person. She was so happy. Her friend was amazed at the instant change in her. She began to cry with happiness and said she felt transformed. Then they had to dash to catch a bus or a train. They said they'll be back.

A 'Reiki Master' came in and I told her about Jesus. She said that her grandmother got saved when she was twelve and prayed with her too. Despite being a master in 'Reiki' healing, she suffered with a lot of health problems. I find it interesting that every time I meet someone who does 'reiki', they almost always have major health problems. Often it's something like fibromyalgia, depression, fear, migraines, arthritis, ME, chronic fatigue or cancer, but they always seem to have debilitating illnesses. When someone involved in 'reiki' lets me pray, they usually feel the power of Jesus strongly and are healed as they renounce 'reiki' ask God to forgive them and tell the demons to leave in the name of Jesus.

I preached at 'School of the Spirit' tonight and the title was, 'Goodbye Wilderness.' At the end of the message I invited intercessors, prophets and prayer warriors to come out for prayer. As we were praying for them, a woman sitting on the back row shouted out, "No, no, no!" I realised it was a demon manifesting. It obviously didn't like the fact we were praying for these people, so I went to the back and helped a few demons to leave her. She began to gag as though she was going to be sick, so someone raced to the kitchen for a bowl just in case. What an eventful day! I'm glad of my bed tonight.

## Thursday 20 May

We're in the United States for two weeks. Last week we took a much needed break staying with my brother and his family in Orlando, Florida. We did nothing but swim, lie by the pool in the sunshine and drink iced coffee. I hadn't had a day off since January as it's been all systems go. It was wonderful and relaxing. Now we're at MorningStar Ministries in South Carolina.

*BBQ at MFM Retreat*

## Friday 21 May

This morning we spoke at MorningStar University and encouraged the students to pray for each other for healing at the end. We had a good time with them, although it was strange being the ones on the stage when we used to be students here ourselves.

## Saturday 22 May

This evening we went for a BBQ with MorningStar friends and walked back to our hotel room at Heritage where MorningStar is based. As the centre of the hotel is where the main meetings are held, we walked past the back of a meeting. We were planning to get a cuppa from the café before going to bed as we were tired. In front of us was a Face Book 'friend' whom I had never met but she recognised us. She reminded me that six weeks ago she wrote on my Face Book wall that there was a prophecy at a MorningStar meeting, "When the people from England come, revival will begin."

As we walked in and she was telling us this, suddenly we heard the speaker (who couldn't even see us) telling everyone in the meeting about his recent prophetic word about the people from England. He said, "Where are the people from England?" Apparently he hadn't met any Brits since he'd prophesied this six weeks previously. The next thing we heard him say was, "Rob and Aliss. Where are Rob and Aliss? Who are Rob and Aliss!?" We reluctantly appeared from behind the back of the elevators and he called us to the stage. He then began to prophesy about a healing stream starting where we are and then he went on to prophesy how the stream is going to increase into a wild, mighty healing river, like white water rapids and run through the UK.

## Monday 24 May

The 'MorningStar Fellowship of Ministries Retreat' began today. At the meeting tonight the speaker called out all the people from Europe. He prophesied that MorningStar would be bigger in Europe than the US and we'd have big events. He then said, "Where are my friends Rob and Aliss?" So again we went forward and he prophesied about a healing outpouring in the UK and that we would be known for creative miracles and new body parts and that we'd have thousands of people saved as a result. He declared that as soon as one thousand were saved through our ministry, then our apostolic ministry would take off, with church planting all over the UK, Europe and Africa. Wowee!! We had a great time.

## Tuesday 25 May

*Ordination at Morning Star*

We spoke at the conference for half an hour this afternoon and shared some stories of the miracles.

Afterwards, many people wanted us to pray for them! Tonight we were ordained for ministry by Rick Joyner. The ordination service began in a serious manner but by the end of it, most of us were on the floor, as the MorningStar leaders went along the line and prayed and prophesied over us. One leader prophesied that I'd write books and they would have a big impact on people. He had no idea that I'm in the middle of writing, 'A Diary of Miracles Part I' telling the amazing stories from our café.

## Thursday 27 May

We're going home today. Just as we were leaving, a Dutch woman approached us and said that she'd watched us speaking at MorningStar University a few days ago in Holland, just before she flew to the States for the upcoming conference. We hadn't realised that the session we spoke at was being watched by people over the world!

At the airport I prayed with a woman whilst we were waiting in line to go through security and her husband leaned over and said quietly, "I'm a freemason". I'm not quite sure why he wanted to tell me that but I replied, "Never mind, Jesus can set you free."

Whilst waiting at our gate at the airport, just before we boarded to fly home, I noticed two women sitting opposite us carrying crutches. They didn't know each other but had got chatting about their injuries and ailments. I couldn't just sit there with them being in pain, so I asked the ladies what was wrong and began to pray for them. They both jumped up and said the pain had gone and were able to walk OK without their crutches. One of them also asked me to pray for her shoulder and her other leg!

## Friday 28 May

We arrived home this morning and then had our 'School of the Spirit' meeting tonight. I'm not quite sure what time of day it is or where I am! We had a good time, although it was hard work setting up the PA system, overseeing the meeting and packing it all away again with missing a night's sleep.

Joy shared that she'd led a lady to Jesus in 'Spirit' shop this week and Margaret said that a Muslim lady had been into the shop and bought a lot of Christian books on prophecy and dreams and had explained that she would like to have a dream interpreted. I wonder if Jesus appeared to her in the dream? I'm hearing about many Muslims who are having visitations from Jesus.

During the meeting tonight, Michael appeared (he's the teenager who prayed a prayer of salvation and was healed last year and who swung the sword over people's heads during worship one evening). He brought eight or ten local lads with him. We prayed over them during the meeting. A guy from North Wales was in the congregation. He came out to the front as we were praying for the lads and told how he had been a drug dealer and alcoholic and had been in prison for many years before he came to know Jesus who set him free and his life had dramatically changed for the better. Michael came forward and knelt at the front and said he wanted to dedicate his life to Jesus. He felt hot, said he was going to cry and then described how he could feel stuff happening on the inside. He did all this in front of his mates.

Adrian (who used to be a medium before he got saved in our café a few months ago) had met a customer called Daniel in the Blacon café and invited him to come to the meeting. Daniel turned up tonight but walked out half way through the meeting. I saw him go, so I followed him out and called him to come back in. I encouraged him to pray out, "Jesus if you're real, show me" so he said it out loud and then he left.

## Sunday 30 May

Our church meeting was quiet, with a lot of people away. But Daniel who'd left early on Friday evening was there. He told me that he'd visited 'Spirit' shop yesterday morning and explained that he had a 'cloud of depression' over him and it left when someone prayed for him in the shop, so he decided to come to church this morning. Then he asked Jesus into his life!

This afternoon we went to a birthday BBQ and I chatted to a guy who told me something encouraging. He said years ago my friend Sue and I (when we were prayer walking around Blacon) had put a note through his door telling him about Jesus. Apparently he'd read the note and then decided to give his life to Jesus. He is now attending a local church. We only put notes through the doors that the Holy Spirit showed us and we hadn't been able to contact him again. God is good.

A Diary of Miracles Part II

# *Chapter Six*

# *June*

"See, I am doing a new thing! Now it springs up; do you not perceive it? I am making a way in the wilderness and streams in the wasteland." Isaiah 43:19

*Shop window*

## Wednesday 2 June

We have to transport a lot of gear such as PA equipment, drum kit and guitars, plus furniture (to sell in the shop), so we need a car with more space. I went to look at a Chevy and a Mitsubishi today in Crewe and bought the Mitsubishi Estate. I hope Rob likes it. We'll have to go back on Saturday to pick it up.

One of our friends told us that he regularly had migraine headaches until he came to hear Charlie Robinson at our 'School of the Spirit' meeting last July. Whilst Charlie was speaking, a spirit causing the migraines left him. He felt it go and hasn't had a migraine since then. Thank you, Lord. I don't think he realised it was caused by an evil spirit until it came out of him! I've discovered that migraines are often caused by evil spirits as well as many other conditions such as chronic fatigue, cancer, fibromyalgia, strokes and scoliosis.

## Thursday 3 June

I was volunteering in 'Spirit' shop again today. A couple came in who didn't know Jesus, but the woman was interested in our miracles after seeing the sign outside. Her husband said he wasn't interested in Jesus at all. However, I prayed with his wife and she began to cry as she breathed in the Holy Spirit. I asked if she was a teacher and she said that she was. Her husband looked surprised! I prophesied to the lady and I know that she will follow Jesus. Suddenly something dropped from the ceiling and a two pence piece rolled towards her husband. I asked if they currently have financial difficulties and she replied, "That's funny, my husband has just been made redundant." We chatted a while and he still wouldn't let me pray with him but I know that the whole experience must have made an impact.

## Friday 4 June

It was quiet in the Blacon café today but such a good day. Two twelve year old boys came in and gave their lives to Jesus. They felt like they got high on the Holy Spirit too. One of them came back later asking how he could get hold of a Bible, so we gave him one of ours. I asked him if he's good at maths and he said that he was really good at it. I told him that I imagine him doing science and maths and formulas. His friend laughed and explained that they had just come back from a trip to the Science Museum in London this week and loved it. I then prophesied to the friend about sport and being an evangelist and doing miracles. He was chuffed.

Just then, another twelve year old boy came in and took one of our leaflets to use as a roach in the end of his cannabis spliff! I followed him outside and he sat on the wall opposite the café with some of his friends.

I began to tell them about Jesus and ended up praying for them. One of the boys said that I'd prayed for his Dad's knee previously and explained how it had been healed and then they all started talking about the miracles that they'd heard about and wanted to know more. One of the lads said his knee had been injured so I prayed and he was really shocked when he discovered the pain had left.

Later on, a guy came past on a bicycle using one hand because he had a broken, 'cracked,' elbow. I told him that if he let us pray, Jesus would heal it. He didn't believe we could do anything to help, but at least he let us pray. We explained that he would be healed and then there would be no doubting that Jesus is real and moving in power today. The pain instantly left and he could move his arm perfectly well. He looked scared and offered us £20! Of course, we wouldn't take his money, but we suggested that he give thanks to Jesus for healing him and to consider following Him.

Mark Buchanan spoke at 'School of the Spirit' tonight on deliverance and then we cast out some demons. A woman came to the front and said she'd had a "pain in the backside" for years. I felt it was a spirit of anxiety that was actually causing her physical pain in her bottom! As we told the demons to leave, she doubled over forwards as each one came out and said she could feel a lot of pain in her back and her wrist. Her right leg began to shake violently and she said she was worried about her new hip! Thankfully, all was well; she was healed and delivered as everyone watched. She said, "Bloomin' cheek! All these years, demons have been causing me a pain in the backside and I never knew." She couldn't stop laughing. A guy got free from a spirit of addiction and felt it come out of his stomach. He left smiling and felt lighter. Hallelujah! Our God reigns.

Sarah told me how a council workman came to do some work at her house and as they were chatting on the doorstep, he explained that he'd injured his arm. She prayed and it was healed, then he gave his life to Jesus. She also said that she'd led the brother of one of our church members to the Lord this week too.

## Wednesday 9 June

There seemed to be a lot of people in church on Sunday morning. We were busy in 'Spirit' shop on Monday and then we went to a prophetic roundtable yesterday.

I was in 'Spirit' shop again today. A woman was browsing our gifts and I noticed she had a bandage on her wrist. She said it was a problem with her tendons so I asked if I could pray for her. She took off her bandage, and as I began to pray she exclaimed, "What's that?" We both noticed what appeared to be a white line like a ribbon appear on her arm, from her finger to her elbow, then it disappeared. She told me the pain had all gone, she could point her finger and raise her arm, something she hadn't been able to do for a while. She said she would go to the pub tonight to play darts now that she can move her arm again! She could really feel the presence of the Holy Spirit.

*A typical sight in the Café*

## Friday 11 June

I prayed with two young women today in the Blacon café who both felt a strong presence of the Holy Spirit. Then I got chatting to some fifteen year old lads outside. One had broken his arm; it was a compound fracture, where the bone sticks out of the skin. He went into all the gory details of what he'd done. I thought he was going to show me a photo! He told me that his mate Michael and our intern prayed with him the other day and now he could move his fingers more. He wasn't completely healed though, so I prayed for him too and the pain left. He could then straighten his fingers. He wanted to know Jesus, so he got saved. He told me he'd already asked his mum to buy him a Bible. Wow! He then told his friend that he'd just given his life to Jesus and said, "Do you want to?" But his friend said "Nah."

Later, Terry Fingers brought in a friend of his with an elongated spine. He said he had too many vertebrae and that it was a generational problem. We prayed for him and he said he needs to get an x-ray but felt something was different. He said if he closed his eyes as we prayed he would have fallen down and said he felt, 'rocky'. Then he asked Jesus to come into his life. We gave him a Bible but he told us he couldn't read as his eyesight was too bad and he couldn't afford glasses. So we prayed for 20:20 vision and told him to try reading again. He could read the Bible easily and said he felt great.

Two women and a guy came in, saying they had driven for over an hour to come to our café. He told us he's been doing missionary work in Africa but he's had to come home as he has some strange illness where his nerve endings are dying and he can't eat. He's very ill and feels suicidal. We prayed for him and broke off any curse, witchcraft etc and suddenly he told us he felt ravenous, ordered a full English breakfast and scoffed the lot. He then wanted to eat what the women had left. He looked like a different person. Amazing! Jesus is wonderful.

Then this afternoon I went to 'Spirit' shop. A couple came in and bought a Mexican sideboard. The husband had a knee problem, so I told him about Jesus and he let me pray for his knee and he reckoned it was healed. They are interested to know more about Jesus and want to come to our meetings.

A friend of ours from America is visiting and we got him to lead worship and I spoke on the river of life. Adrian (who used to be a Medium) got baptised with the Holy Spirit without anyone praying for him and had to drive home intoxicated!

## Saturday 12 June

It's been a good but busy week. The Lord seems to be linking us with people that he's sent from across the country and we're making new connections. Something big is going down!

## Monday 14 June

Our daughter's 17th birthday is today! I can't believe she's that age already. It doesn't seem a moment since she was a toddler.

## Wednesday 16 June

One of our spiritual sons has been arrested for murder and is on remand in a prison in Liverpool. Julia (who was a fellow student at MorningStar when we were there in 2005) and her husband Rob are staying with us, along with their little boy. They live in Brighton and we hadn't seen them for a few years but we got back in touch recently. They're wondering about moving to Blacon to come and help us. Of course, we would love that, but Rob would need to get a job in Chester and as he's a diamond setter he needs to work for a jewellers and we only have retailers in Chester, rather than jewellery workshops or manufacturers.

He had an informal chat with a local jeweller yesterday just to see if they may have an opening for him and they called him half an hour later to offer him a job! Wow! That was quick. Now they're thinking of buying a house up here. I can't quite believe it; that would be wonderful.

## Thursday 17 June

I was working in 'Spirit' shop today. We had two big deliveries of stock, it was very hot and tiring work; unpacking and pricing up all the items and getting rid of the cardboard boxes before customers trip over it all. Linda prayed for a guy with "poorly" eyes. He said they were painful and watery. He seemed to be healed straight away.

## Sunday 20 June

*Julia, Rob and Barney*

Rob and Julia had a great time up here. They're going home tomorrow. Job sorted, house sorted and we took up an offering this morning to bless them and it's enough to pay the deposit on their new house! Thank you, Lord. Everyone loves them. David led worship and the presence of God felt so strong. Sid and Becky are visiting just for today. They used to be part of our church but have been living in Texas for the past year. It was so good to see them.

## Monday 21 June

Wow! Wow! Wow! I was in 'Spirit' shop all day and we sold loads of stuff. I decided to put a sign outside on a black board, 'Today. Free Miracles & Healings.' A couple came in after seeing it and said, "How much for a miracle?" The wife had bronchitis, we prayed and she said she was healed. Then she gave her life to Jesus. It was precious. A whole load of Christians came in too, for a day out. They'd driven quite a way especially to come to our shop.

I popped out for a sandwich at lunch time and as I was walking back to the shop, two women in front of me had stopped and were reading the 'Free Miracle' sign. One had two sticks and could hardly walk, the other had a crutch. I asked what the problem was and the lady with the crutch said she had broken the metatarsals in her foot. She was also wearing a surgical boot. I asked her to sit on a chair we were selling outside the shop and prayed for her foot. She exclaimed, "It's tingling! The pain's gone." Her friend had two sticks and the woman with the broken foot explained that she'd come into town especially to help her friend walk. Her friend suffered from severe arthritis, she was in a lot of pain and needed help walking. They were a picture of misery!!

I asked the woman with arthritis to sit down, I prayed, and then she jumped up and said all the pain had gone. I took her sticks off her and declared, "Walk in the name of Jesus." She walked and was completely healed. Shocked, she walked quite a distance down the street and back again. I caught it on video. She told me that if she stood still her knee would lock and she couldn't get walking again, so she tried standing for a few minutes as I told them the good news about Jesus and then she walked perfectly well without any locking of her knees. Both women gave their lives to Jesus. Well, you would, wouldn't you!?

About twenty minutes after they had gone, a lady came into the shop, picked up a leaflet and said, "Is this where you get your healing?" She explained that she'd been in the women's gym around the corner and the two ladies who had just been healed had gone into the gym and told everyone what had happened. Apparently, until today, they would visit the gym but only for a coffee as they were too ill to use the equipment. However, today they had walked in without using their sticks and had even used the gym equipment! All the other ladies wanted to know what had happened and then asked for the location of our shop so they could get a miracle too. This lady, after seeing her two healed friends, had come in wanting prayer for her family, so we prayed.

Some time later, two elderly sisters appeared and told us they had been to the gym and witnessed the women's healings too. They both needed a miracle. One had a prolapsed disc in her back. It had happened in 1976 and she had been in a lot of pain with her back since, and now in her hip too. She described the pain as being nine, on a scale of one to ten if ten is severe. We prayed and she said the pain had dropped to 'two out of ten' so we prayed again and she said there was zero pain.

Her sister told us that she had severe arthritis in her legs - all the way from her hips down, plus stiffness and a lot of pain. We prayed for her, I told her to jump up, which she did and she was completely healed. She was bending over and walking around the shop with no pain or stiffness. Both then gave their lives to Jesus and took a Bible with them. They explained that when they were young girls they went to Sunday school but have had no experience of Jesus since then, until today!

A customer was watching the whole thing, whilst drinking her coffee. She told us she wasn't a believer but that she'd bought 'The Shack' paperback book from us and read it in our shop and loved it. She enquired, "I have an arthritic knee – please could I have a miracle too?" So she did.

Just then, another woman came in from the gym, telling us that she'd had neck pain for years but didn't have time to stop as she'd ordered food from 'Wok 'n' Go' and she'd be back, but we never saw her again! She must have 'lost her bottle'. Or maybe she'd been healed just walking into the shop. It wouldn't be the first time.

A local artist came in and we prayed for her reflux problem to leave and she felt something happen. Lots of other miracles too, but I can't remember them all. Wonderful Jesus!

## Wednesday 23 June

I was working from home today and received a phone call from the shop. Apparently the two ladies who were healed outside the shop on Monday had been back in. They said the pain in their legs had started to return. I wish I had been there as I would have told them that they need to take authority through Jesus and tell the pain symptoms to leave. This just shows that we need to educate people how to keep their healing.

## Friday 25 June

Rob and Julia had their offer accepted on their favourite house in Blacon, for a lot less than the asking price. I had a lovely relaxing week working from home; writing our newsletter and planning ahead whilst I sat in the warm summer sunshine.

Today in the Blacon café three people gave their lives to Jesus.

The 'Coca-Cola' lady came in with a bad back and could hardly move. She overheard me telling two workmen about the healings and she asked for prayer. All the pain left and she felt warmth in her back. She doesn't live around here but says she goes to church and has been avoiding the evening healing meetings. She said she'll definitely be going now!

One of the young women I prayed with last week was back in today with her Dad who's a taxi driver. She'd told him about the prayer last week and how amazing she felt but he didn't believe her. She told me her life has been so much better since we prayed. Her Dad has diabetes so I prayed while he was waiting for his bacon to be cooked and he said he felt something leave his body! Then they both got saved. He said he could feel cold in his stomach but it felt good. She said her heart felt full. Her dad hadn't been in his taxi since the football started due to a fear of violence, so he prayed and told the spirit of fear to leave and it did. They were both amazed and talking about Jesus. She's going to bring her son in as he has ADHD (attention deficit hyperactivity disorder).

One of our teenage lads whose dad is serving a life sentence in prison came in. He's dropped out of school and has been riding a moped illegally. He had fallen of it and his wrist was all swollen and painful but he hadn't been to the hospital in case someone found out what he'd done. Jesus healed him. The swelling subsided and the pain left. Terry Fingers brought another friend in and he gave his life to Jesus.

'School of the Spirit' was great tonight. Gary Atkins, a local pastor friend of ours, spoke on 'the spirit of poverty'. The Holy Spirit told me earlier today that a couple we know should be moving up here, although they live hundreds of miles away at the moment. I was surprised to see them at the meeting, in fact after I prophesied to them about a move (I didn't say where to as the Holy Spirit hadn't told me to), they told me they were supposed to be going to another meeting tonight but felt they should come to our 'School of the Spirit' meeting instead. They had asked the Lord to confirm their move and were going to ask me to pray into it when I came out and prophesied about it before they said anything.

A lady came to the meeting who had been in our café last year and been set free from many demons. She told me that her life has changed dramatically since that day. Close family who hadn't spoken to her for almost thirty years have been to visit her.

A guy was there who had suffered from serious atrial fibrillation. He had come to our café for prayer a couple of months ago. Soon after we prayed, he had suffered a 'turn' and was rushed into hospital but they couldn't find anything wrong with him. It just so happened to be Easter Day. He explained how his heart has been perfect ever since. The doctors can't believe it.

## Sunday 27 June

The church meeting was great, then we went with our kids to Llangollen as today is Rob's birthday. The weather was beautiful so we sat outside a pub by the river and had some food and a drink and then we paddled in the river and threw stones into the water.

# Tuesday 29 June

Rob and I spoke at a local church this evening. It went well.

*Paddling in Llangollen*

# *Chapter Seven*
## *July*

"…say to the captives, 'Come out,' and to those in darkness, 'Be free!' "They will feed beside the roads and find pasture on every barren hill." Isaiah 49:9

*Boys knuckle healed*

# Friday 2 July

I worked from home for most of this week, catching up on emails and writing 'A Diary of Miracles Part I', but I was in the Blacon café today. I prayed with another taxi driver who had a bad shoulder. He was healed instantly and then he shared how he used to be a homeless drug addict, but one day he prayed to God. Suddenly God appeared to him and he described God as being so bright, He looked like sunshine. As the encounter with God was happening, he realised his hunger for drugs had left and he felt loved. Now this guy lives around the corner from our café, he's married with kids and told me that life's good now that he knows Jesus. His mate told me that I'd prayed for his ankle last year and it was healed and it's still fine.

After the café closed I went into Chester and did a few hours work in 'Spirit' shop. I prayed for a lady who had osteoporosis and was in a lot of pain. She said the pain left and she looked surprised as she told me that surgeons had removed bone from her wrists and put them into her hips, and she'd been told that she would always be in pain, but now it had gone. A couple then came in after seeing the sign outside advertising free miracles. The husband asked if he could have a miracle. He smelled strongly of alcohol and told me he had a bad pain in his back. The doctor had said it was probably arthritis. I prayed and the pain moved to his side, so I told it to go again and it went completely the second time. He actually felt it leave. I think it was an evil spirit.

## Sunday 4 July

It was a weird day today. In the prayer meeting before the service, Linda saw a dark wall we needed to 'punch through' and I felt a demonic presence very strongly during the meeting. I began to feel hot and unwell, my head felt strange, not just as though I was sensing someone near me manifesting evil spirits, but I felt a major demonic presence and had to go outside for some air. I've never felt that before, especially not in church! Towards the end of the meeting, a visitor started screaming and I found her shaking on the floor. I assumed it was an evil spirit and told it to be quiet and to come out. Instantly the woman was quiet, opened her eyes and got up as though nothing had happened. She was a Christian and told me she'd thoroughly enjoyed the meeting! I think she was oblivious to what had just happened.

## Tuesday 6 July

I've been chatting to Roger Forster and Gerald Coates on the phone today. My life is getting even more bizarre.

I'm dreaming of a warehouse that we can use - one day! Sarah rang to say she saw her neighbour who had a bad tooth so she prayed for him and it was completely healed by Jesus. He punched himself in the face to prove it!

## Thursday 8 July

I was in 'Spirit' shop for most of the day and did loads of ministry. A woman came bounding in through the front doors and laughingly announced, "I've come for my free miracle!" I think she was trying to be funny after reading the sign outside, but I said, "Great. What's wrong with you?" She looked puzzled and answered, "I thought it was just a ploy to get people into the shop". Anyway, it turned out that she had a trapped nerve in her shoulder and the pain left the instant we prayed. I asked if she knew Jesus and she replied, "Only in theory, not personally". So I asked if she would like to and she said, "Oh go on then!" She ended up asking Jesus to come into her life after I'd explained exactly what it meant. She said she'll be back with her friends.

Another woman came in. She'd had an operation and was in pain. We prayed and most of the pain left but she told me she wanted to keep some of the pain for some reason, so she did. But she was able to lift her arm a lot higher than before.

A guy came in who claimed to be a Buddhist mystic and told me he doesn't believe Jesus is the only way. I then noticed a woman browsing and she was muttering to herself all the way round the shop. I asked if she would like prayer, particularly for peace of mind and she did. I told the demons they couldn't operate and to come out which they appeared to do and she relaxed. She smiled and said she felt better and gave her life to Jesus. As she left I got chatting to two women outside after I heard one of them complaining about the pain in her side. I prayed and she said all her side went really hard. So I told the stiffness and pain to leave and it did. She was really freaked out by all this and both of them wanted to know about Jesus so I told them about my wonderful Friend. They're very close to getting saved.

## Friday 9 July

Oh glory! I was in the Blacon café today. A young DJ from a local pub came in and after telling him about Jesus he got saved. A workman came in and I began to tell him about the miracles Jesus is doing. He told me that his workmate in the van outside had injured his back and was constantly complaining. He wondered if I could do anything about it. We went outside and he insisted his mate get out of the van which he very reluctantly did, I prayed for him and his back was healed straight away.

A woman came in who had Multiple Sclerosis for 25 years. I told her about the woman with MS last year who got out of her motorised wheelchair in the café and was able to walk after a decade and a half of paralysis. She let me pray and said she could feel heat in her numb toes and explained how her head went fuzzy in a good way. She gave her life to Jesus and then walked unaided to her car!

I bumped into Rhoda crossing the road. She was limping and using crutches. She explained that she'd just had an operation to remove the cartilage from both sides of her knee on Tuesday. When I prayed she felt heat and the pain left. The stiffness also went. She told me she was in hospital yesterday with problems. I recorded her on video as we prayed and then as she walked to the flats above the shops, up two flights of stairs without her crutches and with no pain. She exclaimed, "Jesus Christ!" she was so shocked and I said, "Yes that's the one who healed you."

Amazing day. Amazing Jesus.

*'I can't believe it!'*

# Saturday 10 July

It was the Blacon Festival today. It's a lot of hard work: Rob and Judith were both face painting all day and I was chatting and praying with people. We're always exhausted by the end of the festival, but it's a great way to minister to people. We have queues of parents and children waiting in line, and while they're waiting for their faces to be painted, I chat to them and prophesy and ask if anyone would like prayer for healing.

*Blacon Festival*

There were a lot of healings today. We came across many young people with broken bones. Each time we prayed, they told us the pain left and each was able to move the previously broken limb. Sophie came and chatted to us. She's the young mum of the little girl who was healed of a lazy eye last year in the café. The little girl was there and we could see that the eye was still perfect. I took some video of Sophie sharing how her daughter had a severe problem with her eye. The doctors were convinced she was blind, but Jesus had healed it, the eye instantly went straight, the eyelid opened and she can still see perfectly through it, one year later. Sophie had given her life to Jesus as a result. Her partner came over later and he gave his life to Jesus too.

*Sophie at Blacon Festival*

Just then, a woman on crutches hobbled by. She explained how she had torn the muscle under her foot whilst jogging and was in a lot of pain. We prayed and she was instantly healed. I took video as she showed how she could walk without pain and without the crutches. Both she and her daughter gave their lives to Jesus. Her granddaughter is eleven months old and completely blind, so we reached over into the pushchair whilst she was sleeping and prayed for her. She stayed asleep so there is no way we can know if she's healed yet.

## Monday 12 July

I spoke at a 'Women Aglow' meeting this evening. Just before I left to go there, I was sitting in our living room at home and asked the Holy Spirit what he wanted to do this evening in the meeting. Immediately, two woodpeckers appeared in the tree outside the window. I thought that was quite unusual and it reminded me of the incident with a woodpecker that I'd had a couple of years ago.

*(One day, a friend of mine came to my house for a coffee. I went to put the kettle on and she popped to the cloakroom. As I got up, I felt dizzy, I had a pain in my head, my ears became deaf and I couldn't see properly. I thought I must have stood up too quickly, but as my friend came back into the room, she described the very same symptoms happening to her at the same time. We decided it must be a demonic attack, so we prayed together and told it to leave. As she was talking, I could only see half my friend's face. It was very strange. Most of the symptoms left after we prayed, apart from the fact that we both had a bad headache.*

*After a while my friend went home, but the pain in my head grew worse. I knew it was an evil spirit causing it, so I stood up and commanded it to leave in the name of Jesus. As I did so, there was a loud bang on the upstairs window and a woodpecker fell to the ground, dead, outside the patio windows near where I was standing. I was astonished. I realised that the evil spirit left me, entered the woodpecker and caused it to die. The bird was on its back with its legs in the air, it looked very dead as though it had broken its neck. Now, I like birds, but I don't like to touch them. I wanted to raise it from the dead but wondered if I was supposed to lay hands on it and I didn't want to. I was debating this for a few minutes before I did anything.*

 *I remained inside, looking out through the patio windows and didn't touch it, but I spoke out loud and said, "I command the spirit of death to leave this bird now, in Jesus' name." Instantly the bird's body came back to life, it turned over and stood up, blinking its eyes at me. I could hardly believe it and laughed out loud, however the woodpecker remained there for at least five minutes. I thought it would be ironic if a cat came around the corner and gobbled it up, so I said, "In the name of Jesus, fly." It flew off into a tree.)*

So, the fact that two woodpeckers appeared in the tree straight after I'd asked the Holy Spirit what He wanted to do this evening, made me think that maybe there would be someone at the meeting who had similar symptoms.

I told the story of the woodpecker this evening and then asked if anyone had similar symptoms to those that I'd had, and I wondered if there could be two people (since I'd seen two woodpeckers). Two ladies put their hands up, so I called them out to the front. They told me they had both been suffering from headaches, deafness, dizziness and blurred vision; one for a few days, one for a number of weeks. I explained it was just evil spirits causing it, so they prayed and asked God to forgive them for allowing the evil spirits to have a place in their life and told the demons to go. They both felt something leave and were completely healed; their hearing came back, headaches left and they felt well.

A woman had a lump in her neck and it disappeared when we prayed, plus, when her husband came to pick her up at the end of the meeting, his neck and back were healed too! Another woman's back was healed while I was praying for someone else's!

I heard that a historian has come up with a theory that the site of King Arthur's roundtable was most likely to have been at Chester amphitheatre! It was on Fox News and was also the top story on the news website someone gave me a link to. The next story down was that Britain reveals its new stealth bomber. The Lord's been talking to me about intercession covering us and giving us the ability to move in secret, like a stealth bomber. Interesting.

# Tuesday 13 July

Wow! I wasn't supposed to be in the café today but Shelley was at a funeral. I couldn't find any other volunteers but also I felt the Holy Spirit wanted me to be there today. The young lady who got saved a couple of weeks ago with her taxi driver Dad came in. She told me how her Dad has changed. She said he's stopped swearing and no longer has anger outbursts!

A guy drove for two hours especially to visit the café. He said he's been in two or three times previously, but I hadn't met him. He told me of his guilt, he had left his wife and, I think, has had an affair. He was weeping and asked me to help him give his life to Jesus, so we prayed together. It was wonderful to see him get free from guilt and wanting to get right with God.

Two of our regular guys came into the café but one of them was becoming very aggressive towards the other. I recognised it as being demons (he asked Jesus into his life but doesn't want to get free), so I told the demons they had no power whilst he was in the café, in the name of Jesus, and immediately he changed and became calm.

I got chatting to a girl who was sitting on the wall opposite the café. She told me she'd been in hospital for the past two weeks in a diabetic coma. I prayed with her and told her about Jesus and she asked God to forgive her sin and invited Jesus into her life.

Adrian brought his boss into the café for lunch. Adrian has been following Jesus for about nine months now and his boss told me how she has seen a huge change in him since that time. She'd come because of the change she'd witnessed and to find out if all the miracles she's been hearing about were real. She had a problem with her arm so we prayed and she witnessed a miracle in her own body; her arm was healed.

A young teenager was sitting outside on his bicycle with a bad knee: that was healed. Wonderful day all round! Wonderful Jesus. My sister, brother-in-law and four children are visiting from Northern Ireland, so they came round for dinner. It's great to see them.

## Thursday 15 July

I had emails from Jonathan Helser and Kevin Prosch today. Both are amazing worship leaders, and they're coming to Blacon!!

I was volunteering in 'Spirit' shop this morning. An elderly gentleman saw me putting our 'Free Miracles' sign outside and we got chatting. He told me he had a bad leg so I prayed for it and he said it was better and no longer needed his stick. He offered me money but I wouldn't take it. He kept insisting and gave me £10 to put as a donation towards our work, so that's what I did. It was really kind of him. An older couple came into the shop and I discovered that the wife had suffered a broken leg which hadn't healed and she was in constant pain. After prayer, she said there was no more pain.

A young man in his twenties appeared in the shop and asked to have his chakras aligned (in Hinduism, Buddhism and New Age practices, chakras are thought to be sources of energy in the body). I said, "Come on, I'll sort your chakras out for you!!" Joy and I began to tell him about Jesus and we asked if he'd like to experience the heavenly realms through Jesus. We explained that Jesus is the way and the door to the supernatural realms of heaven, and that it is dangerous to try and use other doorways into the spiritual realm. He said he needed peace in his life and we told him that Jesus is the Prince of Peace. He asked Jesus to forgive him but he said he wasn't ready to give his life to Him yet. Anyway, while we prayed with him, he seemed to experience some travelling in the spirit realm with the Holy Spirit, he began to sweat and seemed to like it and he said he felt stuff happening. But he still believes that all roads lead to God. Lord Jesus, please show him the Truth.

A customer had a pain in the neck so I prayed for it, but it was only slightly better. I asked Joy to pray and when she did, the man was healed completely.

We have the Jourdens arriving tonight. They are a family of six who are American missionaries in Zimbabwe. We just heard that their bus has been delayed so they won't be arriving until after midnight.

I'm in bed; Rob's going to pick them up with another couple from church as we'll need two cars.

## Friday 16 July

We had a busy day in the café, mainly praying for Christians who needed healing and deliverance. We have a lot of Christians come for ministry, although really the café is there to demonstrate God's love and power to people who don't know Jesus and then to mentor and equip them once they're saved. Some people had driven up from South Wales and they got free of demons. A few of them came out fairly loudly in the café which was packed full with customers! One had a serious problem with her jaw and the pain left when we prayed.

Two women came from the North of England for advice and prayer. I prayed for some locals; one of whom I'd prayed for recently for eczema and then he gave his life to Jesus. He told me the eczema is better and he gave up smoking weed sixteen days ago.

The Jourdens came into the café just as we were closing and helped us give out leaflets for our free BBQ on Sunday. A woman was chatting to a local guy we know who's an alcoholic and as we spoke to her about Jesus she began to cry. A close relative of hers has been charged with murder and she's very worried. We were able to pray for the whole situation, for justice to be done and for peace for her and her family. Both she and her daughter gave their lives to Jesus.

We posted invites into a lot of the houses around the café. We gave one to a man who came out of his house and told us he had a large abscess on his gum, a big painful lump. So we prayed for it and it shrank to nothing and the pain left. He was gob smacked!! He said, "Wow. How did you do that?" We told him it was the power of Jesus.

I cooked dinner for ten of us tonight. Then we went and set up for 'School of the Spirit' which was packed out full of people. We had such a good time and eventually got home at midnight. There was a lot of ministry which was great, so Rob and I cleared up and took down the PA system and the chairs while it was going on. We still take all the PA gear and instruments, set up, do the meetings and ministry and put everything away at the end every single week, in fact twice a week. One day hopefully we'll have our own building and more people to help. Keeps us humble though!

A young guy in his twenties wore glasses and explained that he had a lazy eye and he asked us to pray for him. It straightened and he could feel the muscles strengthening as it moved. Thank you Jesus!

### Saturday 17 July

We took the Jourdens into Chester and popped into 'Spirit' shop before showing them the sights. Four teenagers came in, around thirteen years of age. They came up to me and enquired, "Can you tell us about the miracles that take place in here?" I asked how they knew and one of them explained that his mother had popped in on Thursday while she was waiting for the guitar shop next door to open. She saw me praying for the elderly man with a stick who could hardly walk and then she witnessed him put the stick under his arm as he walked off, healed by the power of Jesus. She didn't know anything about Jesus, but she'd gone home and told her family all about it. So her son and his friends came in today to find out more.

I told them that I was happy to talk about the miracles, however, I'd much rather just do one, so I asked if any of them had a pain or an injury. One boy, Andrew, showed me his knuckle and explained that he'd fallen off a trampoline and broken it. It was on his right hand at the base of his index finger. I could see that instead of sticking out as usual, his knuckle was flat, he was unable to make a fist and said he was in a lot of pain. So I put my finger on his knuckle and told his friends to gather round. As you can imagine, being inquisitive teenagers, they closed in so as not to miss anything and I began to pray. Brian got all of this on video.

I took authority over the broken bone and told it to reconstruct in the name of Jesus. Immediately it began to move under my finger and Andrew let out a gasp. He could feel it moving too and his friends witnessed it happening. The bone reconstructed and when we looked properly we could see it had changed shape and appeared to be in the proper position. Andrew said 'wow' as he clenched his fist and told us that all the pain had gone. He then began to punch his friend on the arm; I told him to stop or else we'd be praying for another healing!

They were all shocked and wanted to know about Jesus and then wanted to get saved. So I explained what it meant and we all held hands, standing in the middle of the shop. One of the boys said he was scared so I asked him why. He responded, "When Jesus comes into your life, does it feel weird when He comes into your body?" I replied that it might, but it's 'good weird'. He said, "Oh that's OK then." As we stood in a circle all holding hands and praying and the teenagers gave their lives to Jesus, Andrew, who was holding my hand, suddenly jumped and pulled his hand away. He shrieked and exclaimed that he felt electricity shoot up his arm from my hand. The power of Jesus was moving strongly. They all went light headed and said they felt weird but good. They were all freaked out!

Just then, a man who was walking past the shop had noticed our sign for 'Free Miracles' and came in to ask for prayer. He told us he had damaged his ankle playing sport but wouldn't know if it was healed until he tried to play football again. So I turned to the newly saved teenagers and told them that since they now have the same Holy Spirit living in them that raised

Jesus from the dead, would they like to do the miracle? They readily agreed and two of them bent down and placed their hands on the man's ankle. They prayed, "Please Jesus heal this man's foot – 10, 9, 8, 7, 6, 5, 4, 3, 2, 1 blast off!!" Well, there isn't any formula is there!? Perhaps that was the way Jesus used to do it!

*Teenagers pray for guy's foot '10, 9, 8...'*

We wandered into town with Brian and Pamela and their kids. We met a couple of student girls selling 'Rag Mags'. We weren't interested in buying their Rag Mags, but got chatting to them and they told us they were both on "spiritual journeys". So we prayed and prophesied over them.

One of Brian and Pamela's daughters had earache and a sore throat, so we prayed for her and the pain disappeared.

Our son's computer 'died' a while ago and he's tried everything to get it going again. He hadn't tried praying for it, though. That is, until this evening when he laid hands on it and said, "God, Sorry I haven't spoken to you for a while, but please will you make my computer work?" He went downstairs for a couple of minutes and when he went back it was on and working fine! That made us all laugh.

## Sunday 18 July

We had a great time this morning at church with the Jourden family, then a BBQ afterwards. We do this every few months; we cook huge burgers and sausages and give them away free to the people who come from the community. We got chatting to some people, told them about Jesus and offered to pray for anyone who needed it. Three teenagers gave their lives to Jesus while they were eating their burgers. A young guy had a bad knee and that was healed. Another guy who had come with his girlfriend also had problems, this time with both his knees and he was healed too. A man with sciatica told us the pain left as we prayed. We prayed for someone with cancer but she said she'd need tests before she knew if she was healed, although she felt something happening.

A man who'd had a heart attack let me pray for his heart and he said it started pumping really strongly as we prayed and his eyes welled up with tears as he felt the love and power of God. We also prophesied to some families. A good day all round. Thank you, Jesus.

### Thursday 22 July

Margaret, our Shop Manager, and I went to visit two of our suppliers. They both have huge warehouses packed full of furniture and gifts. I would love to get a warehouse and stock more furniture. Dreaming… One day!

### Sunday 25 July

It's been a tiring week but I haven't needed to work in the shop at all this week and only in the café one day as we have such good volunteers and staff. I prayed for someone's wrist and it was healed plus a woman with spondylitis (inflammation of the vertebrae) said all the pain left. The Jourdens stayed all week in the end.

Something is in the air; something big. I sense angels marching in the tops of the trees, there seems to be a lot of angelic activity. There's a strange light and wind outside, it's weird.

### Saturday 31 July

It's been a strange week. I've been in the Blacon café

most days as many volunteers are away now it's the summer holiday season.

I don't sleep much and I've been praying in the night a lot recently. I'm asking the Lord for words of knowledge and healing angels like William Branham had in the 1940's healing revival in the USA.

Rob is walking up a mountain today with other men from church. I didn't lead anyone to Jesus this week and there have hardly been any healings either. I prayed for a baby's lazy eye three times but nothing seemed to happen. I also prayed for a workman who is going blind and he said there was no change after I'd prayed. I'm asking the Holy Spirit why. Partly there aren't as many miracles as we now spend quite a lot of our time in the café mentoring the new Christians. Many of our customers have been healed so we have less people needing a miracle, but they do need mentoring. We need more people, like 'Fathers' and 'Mothers' who can pastor these new followers of Jesus.

I could do with a break. I'm tired but we can't get enough volunteers at the moment, so I think I'll just have to try and keep going. "Please Lord, send more volunteers and increase sales so we can employ someone for the shop. Thank you!"

I wrote all that in the morning, then walked to 'Spirit' shop where I worked all afternoon. Beth came back in (she got saved along with three teenage boys recently when Andrew had his broken knuckle healed). She brought her friend Donna who had painful lumps on her knee that hurt when she walked. I think it's known as 'Osgood-Schlatter' disease. I gave Beth my phone to video the miracle which she did. I prayed for Donna's knee and the lumps disappeared, so did the pain. She was walking around fine. Then Donna gave her life to Jesus. Both girls felt the presence of the Holy Spirit but Beth began to get a headache so I told her it was just something bad leaving (an evil spirit), then I told it to go and it did. Beth then told me how she'd prayed for another friend on the bus who had a headache and how Jesus had healed him. I suggested a church to them near where they live.

The Holy Spirit gave me words of knowledge for some customers and I prophesied to them this afternoon. Two older ladies said they wanted to give their lives to Jesus. They did so and said how peaceful they felt and how wonderful it was. I suggested they attend a church local to them where they live in Ellesmere Port.

I asked a young woman if she was a teacher and she said, "Yes". I'm glad I got it right; it's always risky getting words of knowledge! She then let me pray with her and she felt the presence of Jesus strongly. Margaret prayed for a lady who had come into the shop after seeing the sign outside for miracles and her back was healed. Then another woman came in and told me I'd prayed for her ankle two weeks ago and the swelling went down immediately. I prayed for a lady with lupus (the name given to a collection of autoimmune diseases). Her arms were red raw and her chest was also red. As Margaret prayed for her we watched the redness on her neck and upper chest disappear. Wonderful Jesus.

# Chapter Eight
## August

"Call to me and I will answer you and tell you great and unsearchable things you do not know." Jeremiah 33:3

With Ian Clayton

# Monday 16 August

Well, I managed to get a break from working in the shop and café for a couple of weeks! I do miss both places when I'm not there though. But I've been writing my first book, "A Diary of Miracles" and have just finished the first draft! My mum is editing and proof-reading it. I decided not to try and find a Publisher as I've heard that most of them are busy and my book wouldn't be published for a year or two. As it's a diary, I need to get it printed as soon as possible, so we've decided to publish it ourselves. I have no idea what it involves, but I'm looking into it. Also we have no money, and we'll need some of that to get a few thousand copies printed. Lord, I'm trusting you for the money.

I've just come back from a couple of days in Cardiff. I went to visit my friend Justin Abraham and he was hosting Ian Clayton, a Christian mystic from New Zealand, so it was good to spend some time with them both and talk about spirit travel. Whilst I was in Cardiff, a couple gave me a gift of money. Wow! I think that's the first time anyone's ever done that for no specific reason, they just wanted to bless us. They had no idea that we 'live by faith' and don't take a wage. God told us He would provide everything we need if we simply follow Him, and that is what is happening. It's a scary journey, but very exciting!

In Cardiff I was invited to visit a small church in someone's home and they asked me to speak about some of the things that we are seeing Jesus do in Chester. I then prophesied that revival would break out in the square in which they live. We all went outside and began to chat to some neighbours who were in the square. One woman said she had a lot of serious health issues. Another neighbour came over; the Lord began to heal her and when I asked, "Do you want to know Jesus?" she started to cry, asked Jesus into her life and was filled with the Holy Spirit. She then declared, "We need a gazebo here every Sunday" which is what the church members had already been discussing!

## Thursday 26 August

Kevin Prosch and his band are all staying with us this week. Arriving with a knock at the door, I was greeted by four people, one of whom was singing 'Alice's Restaurant' on the door step. I realised that must be Kevin!

I worked in 'Spirit' shop today for the first time this month. Kevin, Fergus, Martin and Bekah came in. A guy sitting in the coffee area was in pain with osteo-arthritis so I got the band to help me pray for him. He said the pain was in his ankles, knees and back and was due to cancer. On a scale of 0 to 10 he told us the pain was as severe as it could be, 10 out of 10. I think the cancer treatment must have caused the osteo-arthritis. As we prayed, the man told us the pain diminished from 10 to only 3 on the pain scale, so we prayed again and he said he was completely pain free. He and his wife were amazed and, as Fergus and I held their hands, both gave their lives to Jesus. His wife was glowing and they both described how they could feel the presence of Jesus and felt wonderful on the inside. The couple are from Liverpool so I suggested a church to them that is led by friends of ours.

*Kevin and Fergus outside the shop*

I saw a guy at the till paying for an item and I noticed he was in pain so I enquired what the problem was. He told me that he'd pulled a muscle in his back; he couldn't bend and was in constant pain. Martin and I prayed but nothing happened, so we prayed again and the pain completely disappeared and he was able to move normally with no pain. I said, "Do you want to know Jesus?" to which he replied, "No, he can just heal my back thanks." I prayed that God would keep after him and not let him go.

We prayed for a lovely older lady with dementia and she and her daughter both burst into tears. She made me laugh though; she was asking if we had any books by Rowan Atkinson! I explained to her that Rowan Atkinson was Mr Bean, and did she mean the Archbishop of Canterbury, Rowan Williams?

Just then, two other women came into the shop. One wanted to know if we did "mental healing" after seeing the sign outside for free healing and miracles. I invited her to come and sit down in the coffee shop area. She told me she'd suffered from a broken heart after a relationship ended. I sensed she also had depression and other problems and told her I thought it was caused by an evil spirit.

I explained that we could tell the evil spirit to leave and she would feel better for a time, but if she had not given her life to Jesus and had the Holy Spirit living on the inside of her, then the evil spirit may go and find some demons and bring them back and she'd be worse off. So I asked, "What would you like to do?" She told me that she'd like to give her life to Jesus. So I introduced her to Jesus and explained what it means to give your life to Him. Then I suggested she tell God that she was sorry for going her own way in life and sorry for giving depression and all the other things a place in her life. So she did that and then renounced the evil spirits and told them to leave. She invited Jesus to come into her life and as I watched, I was aware of evil spirits leaving her and the Holy Spirit coming in. She was so happy and crying all at the same time! Her mind seemed still and she felt peace and love.

Her friend then told me that she had eye problems and was also hard of hearing. Even with her hearing aids in she couldn't hear what I was saying. We prayed, she removed her hearing aids and I began to talk to her quietly and she could hear everything I said! Oh, I love it when deaf ears open. They are both interested in being mentored.

A friend of my mother's came into the shop with a bad back. I prayed and she told me the pain went.

A guy in the shop told me he'd had constipation for days. We prayed and told him to be "loosed in the name of Jesus!" Suddenly he exclaimed, "Something's happening, I need to go" and raced off home as fast as he could. I think we had instant break through!!

Back home, I cooked dinner for Kevin Prosch and his band. They are such easy going, friendly guys and full of fun. They filmed a hilarious video featuring our toilet and put it on Face Book. My life is surreal.

# *Friday 27 August*

*Kevin and the band*

Kevin and his band led worship tonight at 'School of the Spirit'. It took us all afternoon to set up. We moved the chairs out of the way so people could dance. We had a great time of worship with them, but half way through the evening, Kevin's voice started to go. He had a sore throat and he told us they'd have to stop the worship. We couldn't let that happen so I started singing as they played. I don't have a singing voice that anyone would like to hear down a microphone but something came over me and I started to sing. I tried to hold it in but it came out anyway when I had the microphone in my hand! I was so embarrassed. Then Rob sang and Sergio, a Spaniard with a great voice, continued. It worked out fine in the end and we all had a great evening.

## Sunday 29 August

We launched our first meeting in North Wales this evening in a hotel near Holywell. Kevin, Fergus and Martin led worship – what a great way to begin our meetings there! We all had a wonderful time.

## Monday 30 August

I'm still freaked that we had Kevin Prosch and his band staying with us for nearly a week. They left this morning to fly home.

*Kevin in Spirit shop*

# Chapter Nine

# September

"Praise the Lord. Give thanks to the Lord for He is good; His love endures forever."
Psalm 106:1

*A popular gift from our shop!*

## Thursday 2 September

I was working in 'Spirit' shop all day today but feeling a bit rough. I'm tired after a busy weekend and my voice is croaky. I blame Kevin Prosch!!

A lady with pneumonia came in today. She's been off work for five weeks and has pain from her lung which she could feel in her back. Jesus healed her completely. All the pain left as she breathed in the Holy Spirit. Then she gave her life to Jesus.

Remember the teenagers who came into the shop after one of their mothers witnessed a man being healed? Well, the mother must have also told a friend of hers about the miracle because the friend came in, wanting to buy a Bible for her mother. We got chatting and she ended up giving her life to Jesus. I gave her a Gideon Bible.

## Friday 3 September

Jonathan Helser and band (Joel, Jake and Chris) arrived today from America. Rob and Adrian picked them up from Manchester airport. We're having a great time with them all. We went to the Blacon café and it was so good to see our staff, volunteers and customers again. I've missed them over August. Our 'School of the Spirit' meeting tonight was amazing. Wonderful music and a strong presence of God was evident. Jonathan Helser is an exceptional worship leader.

*Jonathan and his band in Café Life*

## Saturday 4 September

Viv and Steve got married today. (Viv is the lady for whom I received a word of knowledge about a poltergeist last year and she got saved as a result. She met Steve who also got saved after a word of knowledge and healing at one of our church meetings). My voice has almost gone but I got through the reading at the wedding and people could hear me OK, and Rob gave a short address. Viv and Steve make a wonderful couple.

## Sunday 5 September

We had a great time at the church meeting this morning in Blacon and then also this evening in North

Wales, both with Jonathan Helser and band. What an honour! We are so blessed the Lord is sending all these amazing people to us, without us even asking! When we arrived at the hotel in North Wales where the meeting is held, the room wasn't ready, so we had to wait in the bar. I was chatting to the guys and mentioned that I would like to do a miracle.

A boy walked past us with a bandage on his arm so I asked what the problem was. He told us he'd broken his arm and also sprained it. I suggested to him that we could pray and Jesus would heal it, but I told him to go and check with his Dad first if that was OK. He came back saying yes that was fine. So we prayed and I asked, "Do you feel anything happening?" He replied, "Yes, it's better!" He and his friend then ran and told his Dad, then they both came back, they held hands with me and gave their lives to Jesus. His friend said his school teacher is a Christian so he's going to tell her what happened tomorrow at school. The healed boy said his Dad asked him, "Did it work?" and he said, "Yes" and took off his bandage.

What a wonderful meeting we had; I danced to the music, my ears are ringing, my voice has gone but I'm happy!

## Monday 6 September

My daughter Romany came with me to a 'Ladies Luncheon' in Knutsford today. Knutsford is across the other side of our county, Cheshire, and is quite an upmarket place. I was the guest speaker. My voice was almost gone and when we arrived I realised I'd forgotten my notes. Over lunch I was telling Romany that I would struggle to speak, even though there was a microphone. She said, "Open your mouth and catch this" and threw an invisible fireball at me. I felt something land in my mouth which caused me to fall backwards but when I tried speaking I realised my voice had come back! I spoke for two solid hours without any problems.

Not long after I had begun speaking to the ladies, I was aware of a commotion in the far corner of the room. I tried to ignore it and carried on talking about Jesus and telling some miracle stories. But then I heard a couple of the ladies beginning to call out, "Aliss, Oh Aliss" and their cries were becoming increasingly louder and more hysterical. So I placed the microphone onto the lectern and walked towards the back of the room. The lady with the guitar who'd opened the meeting got up again and started to play, wondering what was happening. So was I!

I discovered a woman lying on the floor looking as though she may have just died. It was hard to tell and I am no expert! A couple of women were trying to get her into the 'recovery position' and another lady was just about to call an ambulance. I had to think fast so I asked the Holy Spirit what to do. I thought it was odd that it had just happened as I began to talk about the power of Jesus, so I guessed it was probably an evil spirit manifesting. I said to the women, "Go ahead and put her in the recovery position if you would like to, but don't call an ambulance just yet, I'm going to cast a demon out of her." You should have seen their faces! I quickly bent over and told the demon to leave her in the name of Jesus. Immediately the woman on the floor sat up. She seemed fine and wondered what was going on. Everyone looked relieved.

I had the attention of the whole room as I made my way back to the lectern and continued with my talk. At the end of the message, I called people forward for prayer. The same woman who'd been lying on the floor came up and asked me about the demons I'd cast out of her. She told me she hasn't been a Christian for long and is going to be baptised next Sunday. I sensed that there were a few more demons that were ready to leave her, so I asked if she would like me to pray with her. I placed my hand gently on her shoulder and told the evil spirits to leave her. As soon as I had spoken, she flew backwards about ten feet as though some invisible force had pushed her, but then stood up with a smile on her face and told me she was free.

Another woman came out for prayer. She had 'polymyalgia' - pain all over her body and feet that were always cold. As we prayed, all the pain left her body and her feet warmed up. Another woman had a dislocated shoulder and couldn't move it. We prayed, held her hand and lifted it up in the air and she exclaimed that she had no pain anymore and her shoulder was as good as new. She certainly couldn't have raised it before. She began to dance and moved her arms all over the place.

A lady with arthritic knees was healed and moving freely. I asked if there was someone near to me who felt "chills" and a woman responded, saying she regularly felt cold in her spine, like someone had "walked over her grave". I told the evil spirit to leave, it went, and her spine became hot.

I then said to the room full of women, "The Holy Spirit has given me the name 'Naomi'. I think it's probably someone's daughter or granddaughter. Everything is going to be OK and it's linked to someone being healed." The woman who had the chills turned to me and said that her daughter was in the room and she'd miscarried a baby called Naomi, in fact she'd had many miscarriages and needed healing. So we prayed with her daughter and I trust she will go on to have healthy babies. Wow. The name was associated with her granddaughter and daughter. Romany helped me pray for everyone.

Went out tonight for a curry with Jonathan Helser and band. They made us laugh. Good times.

Rob and Julia are moving up from Brighton to Blacon, Chester this coming weekend. They'll be staying with us from Saturday until their house purchase goes through. It's amazing to think that they're moving up specially to help support us. God is so good. He is faithful.

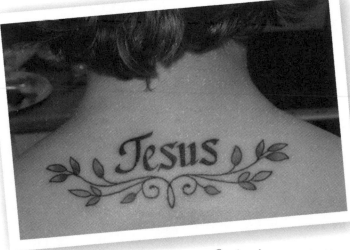

*Julia's new tattoo*

## Wednesday 8 September

Margaret and I drove to a trade show today, looking for new suppliers for our shop. We were on one stand and saw a sign saying, 'Expect a Miracle' so we ordered a few and I told the sales rep that we have miracles. She was desperate for one so we prayed for her and she was weeping. She told us she knows Jesus so we prayed for her to encounter Him in a new way. She was so blessed and couldn't get over it!

# Tuesday 14 September

Happy Birthday to me! It was a bit odd today. Every day is like a birthday for me, so it's always hard to think of something special to do, but I decided I wanted to take Rob to one of our suppliers and buy some nice things for myself - pictures or something. We drove for a couple of hours and when we got there they wouldn't let Rob in. They said his name wasn't on the members list. I told them we're married, both directors of the company and so on but they still wouldn't let him in. Then I said it's my birthday and we'd just driven two hours but they weren't budging. So we drove to another supplier nearby and went there instead. But that wasn't as good, so I tried calling the first supplier and managed to get through to a Manager and explained it all to them. They said it was no problem, they put Rob's name on the list and so we went back again. The original woman wasn't going to let us in again, but when I told her to look on the approved list, Rob's name was on there. She looked shocked but had to let him in! It's all very strange. Anyway, we went round the warehouse and all the things I wanted to buy were out of stock, so I didn't get anything for my birthday. It's probably just as well as we don't really have the money anyway!

# Wednesday 15 September

Good birthday present: Ray Hughes, Brian and Ramey Whalen! They just turned up for a one off event we did in North Wales. The place was full of people. What a great evening!

## Friday 17 September

Rob and Julia have been staying since Saturday. They're buying a house close to our café in Blacon. Very exciting.

I was working in 'Spirit' shop this morning. A lady who had painful shoulders came in. She couldn't move them or lift her arms in the air but Jesus healed her, the pain left and she was then waving her arms above her head.

A couple came in for a miracle after seeing the 'FREE MIRACLE' sign outside. The wife had a trapped nerve in her shoulder and pain all down her arm. It began to ease as we prayed and after telling it to go twice, it was completely healed. I asked if they knew Jesus and they told me they attended a local Methodist Church but didn't know Jesus personally and they would like to, so they both gave their lives to Jesus.

Another couple were in Chester on a trip from Grimsby for a week. They had walked miles sightseeing and the wife's feet were sore. I prayed and the soreness left! Her husband had 'floaters' in his eyes (caused by problems in the eye ball making little grey patches in the vision that appear to float) and the floaters began to disappear as we prayed. As I prayed for his wife's feet I began to giggle as I felt waves of the Holy Spirit, and her husband said seriously, "You're not supposed to laugh." I told him it was the joy of the Lord; that Jesus can give him that and He will give him peace instead of financial worry that is burdening him. He told me that he worries about everything. They both asked Jesus to come into their lives, the husband began to laugh and found it difficult to stop!

Another couple came into the shop after seeing the miracle sign outside. They are locals and also attend a Methodist church and know Jesus. He has lung cancer and shingles with a sore eye and told us his forehead was numb. As we prayed, the numbness left and he said the pain in his eye went too. As we told the lung cancer to leave, he felt waves of heat and cool go through his body and he could breathe better. He has tests on Wednesday that should show if anything's happened.

My mum was working in 'Spirit' shop this afternoon and told me that a young lady came in after seeing the sign for miracles. She had been seeing ghosts and hearing voices. She told my mum she was Pagan but after my mum told her about Jesus, she renounced Paganism and gave her life to Jesus! My mum suggested a church near to where she lives in Chester.

## Saturday 18 September

Rob and I worked in 'Spirit' shop this afternoon with Naomi, a lovely teenage volunteer. Three ladies came in for a coffee and were just on their way out when I got chatting to them about Jesus doing miracles. One had a problem with a facet joint in her back. I hadn't heard of that before, and I think she said there was no gel between some of the vertebrae in her back – she couldn't move much and was in a lot of pain. I asked for a creative miracle, for new facet joints and gel from heaven. It came straight away and she was bending forwards and sideways with no pain at all. Her friends were amazed and said she couldn't normally do that. She then asked if Jesus could also heal the arthritis in her fingers which He did when we prayed.

I was outside the front door of the shop and a lady standing there had pulled a muscle in her neck. We prayed for her, the pain left and she was able to move freely. Then we prayed with a woman who is moving back to Blacon on Monday with her daughter. She's newly separated from her husband and is very worried. I chatted to her for a while and then introduced her to Rob and Julia who have just moved in round the corner from her new place and just happened to walk past the shop at that moment. We prayed with her and gave her a booklet about Jesus.

Two school girls who are doing a geography project came into the shop, wanting to ask some questions about businesses in Chester. In answer to their questions I explained to them how we acquired the shop supernaturally. One of them had anaemia that apparently was causing her hair to fall out. We prayed for her and she said she felt wonderful. The other girl watched and then said she wanted some Holy Spirit too, so we prayed for her and she felt the presence of Jesus strongly.

## Sunday 19 September

David led worship this morning in the meeting, but he was struggling to sing due to the overwhelming presence of God in the room. Our church has been going for three years today! We took up an offering and will donate the whole of the money to one of the other churches in our community. We give to a different church each year to bless them. I preached and then I had a vision of diamonds from heaven. Rob P (being a diamond setter/jeweller) then explained what he thought that meant and we prayed for the young people and children. I love our church family.

## Tuesday 21 September

Randall Cutter, a Pastor from a MorningStar Church down in South Florida arrived today. We'd met him briefly a while ago and thought that since he was travelling back to Manchester airport from Wales, it would be good for him to stop by on his way past. I went to pick him up from the station. As I was waiting for him to arrive, two young women selling cosmetics approached me and began to show me their makeup offers. I decided to buy some of the makeup to give as gifts, and while handing over my money I started to tell them about Jesus and about the miracles we are seeing demonstrated through His power.

One of the girls told me she had knots in her shoulder muscles and couldn't turn her head to the right. The other had back pain. I prayed for them on the station platform and they were both instantly healed, just as Randall approached us. The knots in the woman's shoulder disappeared and she was able to turn her head and the other told us that all her pain had left. I asked them if they knew Jesus and they said they didn't but would like to. So they both prayed and asked Jesus to come into their lives. They said they felt the presence of the Holy Spirit and heat, then they felt Jesus come into their lives.

It was great spending time with Randall and getting to know him better; he took Rob and me out for a meal too!

## Friday 24 September

I was working in 'Spirit' shop today. A lady from Blacon came in after seeing our miracle sign. She said she wanted peace. So I told her about the 'Prince of Peace', Jesus. She then asked the Prince of Peace into her life.

Adam Cates arrived today. He's a wonderful worship leader from Virginia Beach, VA, USA. It's the first time we've met him. He led our 'School of the Spirit' meeting tonight and we had such a good time. Just before the meeting began, a lady who knew Sarah's son Nathan (who committed suicide), said she wanted to end her life but instead she came to the meeting and gave her life to Jesus. A few demons popped out too.

*Rob with Adam Oates*

Late night, we were up chatting with Adam.

### Saturday 25 September

Up early this morning. Adam has been invited to lead a session at a 48 hour worship weekend in Bangor Abbey, Northern Ireland. He had no way of getting from our place to Liverpool airport this morning but it just so happened that we've also been asked to go; Rob is going to lead a worship session too and we found out that we're all booked onto the same flight so we could travel together. The airline doesn't do seat reservations so that worked out fine. We were able to sit together and chat.

The event at Bangor Abbey was wonderful. It was organised by friends of ours, Tom and Iris Ross. It's the valley where St Patrick is said to have camped one night with his followers and they witnessed angels worshipping God. Over one hundred years later at the head of the 'Valley of Angels', also known as Bangor, an Abbey was built on the site and the monks there were well known for their continual praise and worship which lasted 150 years! As we arrived at the marquee today in the grounds of the Abbey, Brian Houston was leading worship. He rocked. We chatted to him afterwards and he gave us a copy of his latest CD. I told him we wanted him to come to Chester if he's ever in the area.

That afternoon in the marquee I noticed Adam on his knees weeping. He'd seen a vision of an angel. I wonder if it was one of the angels St Patrick had seen all those centuries ago.

Adam's evening gig was cancelled at the last minute, so we ended up taking him to a pub and had a great time chatting. Then Rob and I went to my sister and brother-in-law's house for the night.

*Praying at the Bangor Abbey Worship Event*

## Sunday 26 September

We went back to the Abbey today and Rob led a worship session with David Ross, one of our leaders. He arrived a few days ago. So glad we came. We went for a walk around the gardens and then back to my sister's house again. It was lovely to see the family and spend a bit of time with them.

## Monday 27 September

We took the flight back home to Chester today.

# Tuesday 28 September

I worked in the Blacon café today. There seemed to be a lot of ear problems. Rob works two days each week for a local charity and one of his colleagues came into the café complaining of a deaf ear. It was blocked and painful and she had vertigo. We prayed, she felt what she described as a 'wind' in her ear and it opened straight away. We tested it out and she could hear and she said she had no pain. She went back to work and told Rob, "Your wife just healed my ear!"

I got chatting to a man "without a hip" about angels and 'reiki'. He didn't want any prayer. He said 'reiki' healing is all he needs, but I wondered, if that was the case, why he had no hip and was unable to walk properly. Just saying.

I prayed with a woman from Saughall (a nearby village) who had tinnitus (ringing) in her ear. As I prayed she said it started to hurt, then the pain left, then the ringing began to go. She needed it to be quiet to test it out fully and it was too noisy in the café so she's going to go home and let me know another time.

A young woman came in and I asked if her name was Chloe. She said it was. I didn't recognise her but she told me that a few years ago I had healed her kidney. I remembered what happened. It's a funny story. Linda and I were sitting on a wall near the pub and I told Linda a joke: "A man walks into a fish and chip shop and says 'I'd like a steak and kiddly pie please.' The staff member replies, 'You mean a steak and kidney pie don't you?' The customer then says, 'I said kiddly, diddle I?'" Well, Linda was laughing and then I felt there was some other reason why I'd told that joke. I wondered if it was a word of knowledge the Holy Spirit was trying to tell me through the joke.

I know it sounds weird, but I got up and noticed a group of young women sitting at a table outside the pub, having a drink. We wandered over, I approached them and said, "Hi, I'm Aliss. I just wondered if any of you has a kidney problem." They looked startled, but one of them replied, "That's mad! I've got a kidney infection, it won't go, I'm in agony and I was just complaining about it." Linda and I told them about Jesus and how He had sent us, so we prayed for the girl and she was shocked as the pain disappeared. Then she and a few of the others gave their lives to Jesus.

The young woman who had just walked into the café today was this same woman, Chloe. I had no idea what her name was until the Holy Spirit told it me today. She recognised me, although I wouldn't have recognised her. She explained how her kidney was completely healed that day and how she has had no problems with it since.

This evening a couple came to see us who would like to join our church! We need more people to help disciple the new Christians, but we're not so keen when they leave their current church to join with us. At least we have a good relationship with most of the Pastors in the area, so we're able to chat to them about anyone who wants to join with us before they do.

# Chapter Ten
## October

"And He said to them, 'Follow me and I will make you fishers of men'." Matthew 4:19

Moriah Chapel -
Birth place of the 1904 Welsh Revival

## Friday 1 October

I don't feel well today. I have been asked to share at a Women's Conference in Llanelli, South Wales about healing. I couldn't exactly cancel and say "The healing session is cancelled due to sickness" and I know I am supposed to be there, so I've been fighting the infection and telling it to leave in the name of Jesus. I'm learning that often when we need healing ourselves, we really must contend and fight the illness or pain. Then I find it leaves. I rarely get ill but when I do it seems to be when I've been doing too much without a break and not resting as I should. It's difficult when you have a lot of responsibility. Even when I try to rest, the concerns are always revolving in my mind.

I drove to Llanelli in South Wales this afternoon. It took me nearly six hours as the weather was awful and the Welsh roads are slow and winding. I could barely see; the wind was blowing the rain horizontally and it got dark early. But this evening session was so good. I met Sarah Trinder who is the main speaker. She's a Pastor from South Wales and makes us all laugh. We seemed to get on well and had a good chat just before the service.

## Saturday 2 October

We went to Moriah Chapel this morning in Loughor and stood in the pulpit where Evan Roberts preached and where the Welsh Revival of 1904 began. The presence of God felt strong in the little Sunday School chapel next door. We visited Roberts' grave and prayed that the spirit of revival would flow once more in Wales and across the whole of the UK and sweep into the rest of Europe. My great grandfather, Thomas Parry, lived in Aberdare and was eighteen or nineteen years old in 1904. Evan Roberts visited Aberdare only a matter of days after the revival began in Moriah Chapel. I imagined Thomas meeting Evan and hearing him preach, joining with the congregation singing and witnessing the greatest revival that this land has ever experienced. Later my great grandfather went on to become an Elder in the Apostolic Church of Wales that was born out of the Welsh Revival.

My great grandfather Thomas Parry age 19 years in 1904

This afternoon I led a seminar on healing, back at the conference. Before I began, a woman spoke up and told us all that she and her friends were "off healing" since they had prayed for a teenage boy, the son of one of the women at the conference, but he had died. Since then, they couldn't believe that it was God's will to heal people today. They had huge disappointment and many questions. Obviously that made it difficult for me as I began to speak, but it was helpful to know what many of them were thinking! Anyway, I spoke for half an hour or so, still feeling ill, and trying to explain, using Scriptures, that it is God's will to heal, but not all are healed. Just as it is God's will that "none should perish" but that not all are saved. It doesn't stop the fact that it's the truth.

I shared some 'words of knowledge' and asked people to come forward for healing in response. A young woman came out. She told us that she had broken her back ten years ago. She'd had metal plates inserted into her back and had been in constant pain ever since. She explained that it was impossible for her to reach over into the cot and pick up her baby. She was on liquid morphine to try and help relieve the pain and always had to use a cushion when she sat. Life was tough for her.

I spoke to the women who'd prayed for the teenager that had died, and suggested they pray for the young woman with the broken back. They hesitated, but bravely came out and laid hands on her back and began to pray. Suddenly, the young woman began to howl. We wondered what was happening. She was crying and making a loud noise. I realised she was being completely healed. She started to jump around and was squealing. I quickly picked up my phone and began to video her. She told us that she'd felt something leave and that she was out of pain and able to bend for the first time in ten years since the accident. The women who'd prayed for her were amazed. God is sooooooo good. It really brought home to me the fact that it's important not to base our faith on our experiences but on what the Bible says.

*"No pain!!"*

Another lady came forward. She was suffering from arthritis and as we prayed she said all the pain left, she felt tingling and could bend her fingers and knees for the first time in years.

I suggested that the woman who'd had her broken back healed should pray for others, so she began to pray and she was seeing miracles happen. How wonderful.

I had a word of knowledge for someone with problems connected to childbirth and colostomy. A woman came forward who'd had a stillborn baby - she'd had complications and now had no colon and many abscesses in her body. She'd been told that she was going to die. We broke off a curse, she felt it go and said she could feel something happening but she wouldn't know straight away if she was healed. Lord, please heal her.

Just before I left the conference, I met a woman in the foyer who had slipped discs in her back and a trapped sciatic nerve. As I prayed, she said something moved in her back and she was able to bend. All the pain left her.

It was a long drive home in the dark with terrible weather and winding roads, but it was definitely worth it!

## Tuesday 5 October

I was in the Blacon café today. A guy came in early, before we'd officially opened. I served him a cooked breakfast and said, "Can I get you anything else?" to which he replied, "Yes please, a model" (referring to the models that appear in some of the British tabloid press). I told him I couldn't help him with that but I could introduce him to Jesus. So I did. Jesus healed his neck, his twenty year back problem, a chest infection and his asthma. He was able to breathe again! Maybe he'll be able to find a model now!!

Also a lady with an eye problem was healed and a woman who couldn't move her shoulder due to torn tissue was prayed for. She was then able to move it freely with no pain. I got that on video.

## Saturday 9 October

My sister, her husband and four children from Northern Ireland are staying with us. My brother, his wife and their four kids from Florida are staying with my Mum and Dad and then we're having their two teenagers with us for a few days. It was my Dad's 70th birthday party today. We had a Chinese meal and many of his friends and family came. We had a wonderful time with friends and family.

## Sunday 10 October

All the family went for a curry tonight. It isn't often that we all get together since my brother and sister live overseas, so it was a rare treat to spend quality time with them all in one place. My teenage nephew, Josh, was complaining of deafness in one ear and said that both his ears were painful. We prayed and he was instantly healed!

# Tuesday 12 October

A guy came into the Blacon café today and told me he'd just moved to Blacon. He ordered a takeaway breakfast and then Ian who was volunteering told him how Jesus helped him get free from drugs. The guy explained that he used to be a refuse collector but he has permanent pain in his back and is unable to work now. We prayed and he said it felt weird, then he realised all the pain was gone and he was able to bend forwards. He told us he was Catholic, although not 'practicing' at the moment.

Bobby & Caroline came in. I've not seen them since June last year when I prayed for them. At the time, Bobby explained that he often collapsed for no reason and he was wired up for tests by the hospital when we met. He told me that since I'd prayed last year he'd had no more problems until today and he collapsed again this morning! That's weird. But he also said that he'd given his life to Jesus after we met. Caroline has brain haemorrhages but the doctors can't find out where they're coming from. I remember praying for her last year too, but she said they're still happening now and again. Very strange. We broke curses off them. They're such a nice couple and have had a lot to cope with.

Ian told us a great story. He said that on Sunday he was desperately trying to find his benefits cheque. He turned his flat upside down looking for it. He even called his mum to come and help him. He was beside himself as he needed the money urgently. He said he was so desperate that he asked God to help him and heard His voice in his head saying, "Look under the hall mat". He looked under the mat in the hall and there it was! Now he knows what a word of knowledge is!

Rob's away for a couple of nights at the local Link Up churches Leaders' Retreat in Southport. I'm hoping to get my first book, 'A Diary of Miracles Part I' to the printers this Friday. I'm excited. I'm getting 1,000 copies printed to start with. Mum and Dad are lending us the money to do it, and as soon as I've sold enough copies we'll pay them back.

My brother and family (who are over from Florida) popped in with a sleeping bag as they were having a clear out, so I put it under the stairs and told them it'll probably come in useful. My sister and her family are staying. It was great to all be together for my dad's birthday.

## Wednesday 13 October

When I woke up this morning I had a thought that the next time I go to Tesco supermarket someone is going to get healed. Later, I went to B&Q to get a toilet seat, then realised we needed some Panini bread for the café as we've run out so I decided to go to Tesco since it's close to B&Q and I needed a few other things too. I went to get a trolley (shopping cart) by the entrance and got chatting to a homeless man who was standing there. He told me he was in a lot of pain with pneumonia. He was supposed to be in hospital with it. He said he'd had it for weeks and he was finding it difficult to breathe while he was talking and he kept coughing. He looked rough! I suggested he let me pray for him which he did. Within seconds the colour came back in his cheeks, the coughing stopped and he was able to breathe normally. He said the pain had gone too. He was shocked and began to laugh. I told him if he waited there I'd take him to our café for a big breakfast.

So he waited outside whilst I went in and bought the panini bread and the other things we needed. He got into my car and I drove him to the café. We gave him a big breakfast and a cup of tea for which he was grateful. As he sat at the table he shared with others about his healing from pneumonia and I started to take some video of his testimony. He told me he also had 'trench foot' because he continually wore boots and often they would get wet and muddy but he wasn't able to change them. As we prayed he was healed and I managed to catch it on video at the same time. Just then another guy came into the café and said, "If I ever need a miracle I need one now – but I just need to go to the toilet first!" So after he'd been to the bathroom, we prayed with him, he gave his life to Jesus and got free of some evil spirits. He said he felt a lot lighter.

*The homeless guy with pneumonia*

Then the homeless guy told us that someone had stolen his sleeping bag and he didn't know what he was going to do that night as it was cold. I remembered that yesterday my brother had popped round and given us a sleeping bag. How amazing!! I knew it would come in useful.

At 'School of the Spirit' tonight, four teenagers came in off the streets; two of them were girls I hadn't seen before. One said she had a 'clicky' hip and the other had a dislocated knee problem. We prayed and the power of Jesus healed them both immediately. They were really surprised!

## Saturday 16 October

We had a rest this morning and then Rob and I were working in 'Spirit' shop this afternoon. An older lady came in and told us she was a neighbour of someone in our church who had told her about our shop. She said she needed a miracle for her son and granddaughter and as she was unstable on her feet, I suggested she sit down and then we prayed for her family.

I asked why she needed a stick and she explained that her body was riddled with arthritis. As we prayed, she felt the power of God moving in waves through her body and began to cry. When I asked her to jump up, she laughed thinking the last time she 'jumped up' from being seated was as a young woman many years ago. However, she did jump up, easily and quickly. She said normally her knees would lock or give way, but they were normal. She had no pain or stiffness and was able to turn her head sideways for the first time in years. She'd had one hip replaced and told me the other needed doing but that was healed too! She was stunned as she realised she could bend her fingers, something she hadn't been able to do for a long time. She was completely healed by Jesus!

She showed me a large lump on the side of her hand so I placed my fingers on it and told it to disappear in the name of Jesus. It shrank and disappeared as we watched! She folded her stick up and put it in her handbag. Wow!

Later, I noticed three students outside the shop taking a photo of our miracle sign: "Free Healings & Miracles". So I went outside the shop door and said, "Would you like a miracle to go with your photo?" They laughed, but it turned out that one of them had a cigarette burn on his arm, at least the size of a 10 pence coin. It was dark purple and had apparently been there for 2 ½ years. I put my finger on it and told it to go in the name of Jesus. As we watched, it went pale, shrank and a weird line appeared. He was really freaked out!!!

Soon afterwards, two more students came into the shop asking about the miracles. The girl had problems with her head, she told me, and was having tests at the hospital. I asked her if she'd been messing about with a 'ouija board'. She said she often did. I explained to her about the danger of the occult and evil spirits and how that was probably the cause of her physical problems. Standing in the middle of the shop, she asked God to forgive her, renounced what she'd been doing, told the demons to leave and asked Jesus to come into her life, as her friend stood by looking a bit bemused! As the demons came out she felt fuzzy in her head then she exploded with joy as she was filled with the Holy Spirit. She told me she hadn't felt so good in ages.

Later I noticed a married couple outside the shop so I went and said, "Hello". They were from Manchester and had come to Chester for the day, shopping. I explained about the miracles that Jesus is doing. The woman said she'd had a frozen shoulder for fifteen years and she showed me how she was unable to lift her arm any higher than her shoulder. I prayed and asked her to lift her arm up. She put it straight up in the air and was swinging it around! They were both amazed.

Then four young people from Crewe came in. One was on crutches. He said he'd torn the ligaments in his ankle and I could see it was swollen. He let us put our hands on his ankle and his friends were all shocked as they watched the swelling go right down and the pain left. He could move it normally, so he swung his crutches over his shoulder and walked out completely healed by Jesus.

Then another person came in with a 'frozen' shoulder! We prayed for him and he said he was healed. A tourist who was watching asked if we could help her too. She showed us her legs – they were covered with a red, itchy, lumpy rash. She said it had been there a long time and the doctors could do nothing for her. She'd tried everything. So I put my hands over her legs and released the power of Jesus. We watched the lumps disappear and the bright red rash faded to a very pale colour. Suddenly she said she had to go and dashed off to catch her coach!

A lady with bad asthma told us the doctors could do no more for her. She'd been in hospital and found it difficult to talk without wheezing and coughing. We told the asthma to leave in the name of Jesus and asked her to breathe in the Holy Spirit and breathe out the asthma. Instantly she was breathing well, the wheeze and cough seemed to disappear. Wowee!! What a day.

## Sunday 17 October

I spent the evening with my face on the carpet going 'Wooooooaaaaahhhh'! I only managed to get two or three hours of sleep last night as the Presence of God was so tangible, I could feel waves of His glory in the room. Then I saw two bright blue lightning bolts in my bedroom. I was so scared and amazed I didn't want to close my eyes.

This morning at the church meeting I spoke on Gideon and described how an angel had appeared in my bedroom two weeks ago and had placed in my hands a large rusty key and a shining sword. I knew the angel was connected to Gideon somehow. The key he gave me was a key of authority for the UK. It was a key that could lock people or forces of evil out of the country and it could also let certain people and the Kingdom of God into the country. I knew that it carried with it a great responsibility and I was not sure I was ready for what I was being entrusted with. But I asked God to give me humility, wisdom and discernment. I also knew that the key I was given was not by any means the only key to be given out at this time.

*Symbols of Kingdom authority*

The key had not been used for many years, but I was told that as I used it in faith and being led by the Holy Spirit, the rust would disappear. In contrast, the massive sword looked brand new as it glimmered and shone, however, I knew that it too was ancient but was being brought out for this special time in history. I was reminded of Gideon's army who went into battle with only trumpets and flaming torches, and how they shouted, "A sword for the Lord and for Gideon" causing the enemy army to flee and turn their swords on each other! (see Judges 7).

During the meeting, a teenager gave her life to Jesus and then afterwards all the leaders came back to our house for lunch.

## Monday 18 October

I worked in 'Spirit' shop this afternoon. Three Muslim ladies came in because they'd seen the sign about miracles and healing. One of them told me she had fibromyalgia and showed me the support bandages she wore on her arms. Fibromyalgia always seems to be a demon, in my experience, so I put my hand on her head and told it to leave in the name of Jesus. She was surprised as she felt the pain move all down her body and she told me she could feel it coming out of her feet. All the pain had gone.

I asked her if she knew Jesus and she told me she was a Muslim. I then said, "Would you like to know Jesus?" to which she replied, "Yes please." But just before she had chance to give her life to Jesus, an older lady who turned out to be her mother, grabbed her by the arm and said "No, we're Muslim" and marched out of the shop dragging the other woman with her. As they left, I prayed out loud that Jesus would show up in the woman's home and she would give her life to Him.

Two young women came in asking for prayer. They sat down in the coffee area and I asked them what the problem was. One of them told me that she was gay and had recently split up with her girlfriend and she was suffering from a broken heart. So I prayed with her and asked Jesus to heal her heart. She felt something happening and could feel love like she'd not known before as I released the love of God into her heart through the Holy Spirit. I prayed that she'd know Jesus personally and asked her if she'd like to give her life to Jesus. She said she wasn't ready for that today as it would mean some changes in her life but she thanked me for praying and said she felt a lot better.

I got chatting to a customer who had a bad back. Another lady who was browsing our shop overheard our conversation and explained that she had a bad back too. So in the middle of the shop I placed one hand on one back and one on the other and prayed for the two customers at the same time! Both were amazed as the pain and stiffness left instantly and I began to tell them about Jesus. So instead of shopping they were listening intently as I told them how He died on the cross for them and rose again and how they can know Him. Both of them said they wanted to give their lives to Jesus, so the three of us prayed together and they both got saved! Wonderful.

I don't think it's particularly good for business doing so much ministry, but that's what we're there for. I think we lose a lot of sales as we would rather introduce people to Jesus' love and power than make a sale. It's hard trying to get the balance right, but I'm trusting that the money will come in to pay the rent and the bills. If we charged for miracles we'd be making a fortune!! It's a good job we're storing up treasure in heaven where thieves and moths can't destroy it (see Luke 12:33).

Later, a man came into the shop. We told him about the miracles that had just happened and he said he had arthritis in his shoulder. We prayed and he was healed too and could move it without pain. He said he was in agony before we'd prayed. Thank you, Jesus.

## Tuesday 19 October

It was really quiet in the Blacon café today. It poured down with rain all day, so I think the customers stayed at home. I had no-one to pray for, but Ian came in. He had been on heroin for 27 years until he came into our café and gave his life to Jesus. He's doing really well. He spends a lot of time in the café and comes to church every Sunday.

## Wednesday 20 October

In a vision today I saw Jesus walk into my kitchen at home. I invited Him to come and sit down and we chatted for hours. It was amazing. I was unable to speak to anyone for a while afterwards I was so freaked out. He told me some wonderful truths and glowed with a love I have never known before.

## Thursday 21 October

We started employing James today as we managed to secure some grant funding for salaries. I'm really pleased; it's going to make a big difference and free me up a lot.

I worked in 'Spirit' shop until 3pm today. Margaret's on holiday. A woman wanted healing of arthritis in her legs. I prayed but absolutely nothing happened. I mentioned to her that sometimes arthritis is caused if you've been hurt emotionally by someone and you can't forgive them. She replied, "There is no way I will ever forgive them, ever!" Oh dear. She didn't want to know Jesus either. I couldn't do much but I prayed that God would soften her heart. She told me that she's 84 years old.

Another woman came in and told me she was healed last time she came into our shop. This time she had a chest infection so she came specially for healing. We prayed and she said the pain left and she felt better. She'd brought her elderly aunt with her who had lung cancer. We began to pray for her and had to hold her up as her knees began to buckle as she felt the presence of God very strongly.

A friend of the woman who was healed of a broken back in Llanelli told her boss about her friend's healing. He has a bad back and was so amazed by the healing of the broken back that he asked if I'd pray for him too, even though he didn't know anything about Jesus. I prayed over the phone for him and he told me that all the pain left.

Hoping my book is going to the printers tomorrow.

# *Friday 22 October*

I was in 'Spirit' shop with two volunteers today. They were able to lead two ladies from South Wales to Jesus. The women renounced Spiritism and received emotional healing. They were visiting Chester and felt that God had brought them here especially so they could give their lives to Him. We all held hands as they got saved and were filled with joy.

We prayed for a guy with blocked sinuses and deaf ears. His ears opened, he could hear again and his sinuses cleared and all the pain left. He was so pleased. A lady from our church brought two of her friends in. One of them had a condition called spondylitis which caused a lot of pain in his back. He said it was constant and severe. We prayed and he felt the pain move and then leave his body. His wife was deaf in both ears and wore a hearing aid in one. As we prayed her hearing came back! She took her hearing aid out and could hear well. We prophesied to them.

A lady came in with back pain and she was healed and then we prayed with a woman who had diabetes and she could feel something happening as we prayed and could hardly stand up due to the strong presence of the Holy Spirit.

We had a great time at 'School of the Spirit' tonight – Rob spoke about the presence of God.

# Saturday 23 October

Yesterday as I was leaving the shop a woman came in who made me feel uneasy. Stupidly I didn't do anything about it, and thinking back I reckon she was trying to curse us. I arrived in the shop today at 1pm and my mother, who was working this morning, told me that not one customer had come in. That is so unusual, especially for a Saturday which is always busy. So I prayed around the shop and broke off any curse. Instantly customers began to come in!

Julia popped in and then we went outside to chat to three lads from Blacon who were on their bikes. One told us he had a hard bony lump just under his knee and showed it to us. It was quite big and knobbly. We told it to shrink and it did.

Another of the lads had a sore shoulder but nothing happened when we prayed for it. He also had wrist pain and that went. He was really shocked but then it came back again! Not quite sure why. That happens occasionally and so I often tell people that they need to follow Jesus and if symptoms come back they must tell them to leave in the name of Jesus and not let them back. We prophesied to them too.

A guy called Neil came in and told us he couldn't kneel! Or crouch down. He said he'd been in so much pain since he was a teenager. He had a huge hard lump under his knee. We told him that Jesus would heal it, but he said, "I'm not religious. Does that matter? Will it work?" We explained that we're not religious either, we're followers of Jesus. The massive lump on his knee shrank, almost all the pain left when we prayed and he knelt on the floor and was able to crouch too.

Another guy saw what was happening and told us that he had knee trouble too – he needed new cartilage and it felt cold for some reason. We prayed and released new cartilage from heaven. He tested it out and said all the pain had left and it felt perfect.

Then two students came into the shop. One of the girls explained that she had a deformed knuckle. I could see that instead of standing out, the knuckle seemed to go in. It was painful and made a crunching sound when she moved her hand. We prayed and nothing seemed to happen. I prayed again and she said it was exactly the same. She said not to bother again but I wanted to pray one last time. I prayed again and she said it felt funny. She started to laugh and told me the pain left, the crunching stopped and it looked perfect. The knuckle had moved and was now standing out when she clenched her fist. She was so shocked. I asked them both if they knew Jesus and they shook their heads. I asked if they would like to know Him and follow Him and they both said, "Yes please!" So they gave their lives to Jesus and as they invited Him in, they both said they could feel a strange but nice feeling on the inside, one said it was under her ribs. I told them it was the Holy Spirit moving in. Amazing!

I noticed an unusual looking couple outside the shop, looking at our miracle sign. I went to say, "Hello" and he told me that he's a contortionist and is performing tonight in Chester. He showed me how his shoulder came out of joint and looked deformed but he didn't want that healing as he would no longer be a contortionist! But he had a problem with his wrist that needed fixing so I prayed and Jesus healed it. His girlfriend needed new kidneys and had asthma and I asked if she also had panic attacks. She replied that she did. I explained that it was caused by a spirit of fear that had come through her involvement with the occult. She hadn't told me about the occult so she looked a bit surprised that I knew what she'd been up to. I helped her to pray out and she asked God to forgive her and set her free.

A customer was telling me that she suffered with arthritis very badly when I asked why she was limping. I said, "On a scale of 0 to 10, if 10 is excruciating pain and 0 is no pain, can you describe your pain?" She said it was a '10'. We prayed, she moved around and said the pain was now a '2'. We thanked Jesus, then told the rest of the pain to leave and she said she felt wonderful. No pain at all! She told us that she knew Jesus and was just visiting Chester.

# *Monday 25 October*

My first book went to the printers today!!! Very excited and a bit scared.

I went to Morrisons supermarket to do my weekly grocery shop. I was pushing my trolley down an aisle when I noticed a woman walking towards me with a number of children pulling at her and hanging off her trolley. It was spilling over with groceries and she looked a bit hassled. I also noticed that she was wearing a surgical boot, walking with a limp and trying to manoeuvre with crutches too. It's hard to walk past someone in pain or ill when you know that if you were to pray for them they'd be healed.

So I mustered up some courage and asked her if she would like me to pray for her foot which she told me was broken. Unfortunately she didn't want prayer and limped off as quickly as she could with kids, trolley, surgical boot and everything! I was feeling bad and hoped no-one had seen me. I find it difficult approaching someone I don't know and always feel stupid asking them if they'd like prayer. I know it's good for my soul though!

Anyway, I was just feeling miserable and really wanted to do a miracle. An older guy walking past me leaned over and said, "Wow, your hair is lovely, really beautiful". It cheered me up no end! I noticed he had hearing aids in both his ears. I asked him if I could pray but he was so deaf he couldn't even hear me with his hearing aids in. So I thought, "What the heck!" and decided to go for it anyway. I slapped my hands on his ears and commanded the deafness to leave in the name of Jesus. He was startled and wondered what was going on. He took out his hearing aids and told me he could feel vibrations going through his ears. He put his hearing aids in his pocket and could hear every word I said, even a whisper when I stood behind him. Jesus had opened up his ears!

*An ideal place for a miracle!*

Then I noticed that he was using a walking stick. I asked what the problem was and he told me that he had muscle wastage in his hip. I got him to put his hand on it and then put my hand on top of his hand. Unfortunately, it was slightly behind his hip and I realised there I was in the middle of the supermarket with my hand on some guy's backside! I began to pray, but then who should I see bounding round the corner, but his wife!? She exclaimed, "What's going on here then?"

I tried to look as much like a Christian Minister as I could (failing miserably), but she said not to worry, she thought he'd had one of his fainting fits and I'd caught him! Undeterred, I snatched his walking stick from him and ordered him to "Walk in the name of Jesus!" He slowly began to walk down the aisle, then realised he was walking perfectly and began to jog. His wife discovered that he could hear every word she was saying and overjoyed, they hugged and cried, I joined in and we were hugging and crying like long lost friends. How wonderful Jesus is! They told me they knew Jesus but didn't know that He still heals today. But now they do. I told them about our shop and they promised to come and to keep in touch.

## Thursday 28 October

I was working in 'Spirit' this afternoon. A young man came in and told me he'd given his life to Jesus in the shop two weeks ago. He explained how he'd been on drugs and in prison and was self-harming so badly that he'd been in hospital. He suddenly had an urge to self-harm again, but thankfully came into the shop to get help. He knows that now he's following Jesus he doesn't need to do that anymore but is finding it difficult to stop. I explained that it's probably an evil spirit so we prayed and he told it to leave. He was crying and said he felt much better.

Then his friend came in. He wanted to know what was going on and what the wonderful feeling was that he could sense. We told him about Jesus and he got saved too. Then we prayed for his brain tumour to go.

A woman came into the shop after seeing our sign outside. She told us she was suffering from depression, so I explained to her that I could tell it to leave, but if she is not following Jesus it may come back and she'd be worse off than before. So she decided she wanted to follow Jesus. She asked God to forgive her sin, she told the depression to leave and asked Jesus into her life. She was filled with the Holy Spirit and looked radiant.

Later a man came in with exactly the same thing after seeing the sign. I said the same to him and he got saved too!

There were more wonderful miracles today but I can't remember them all.

## Friday 29 October

The young guy with the brain tumour who got saved yesterday came back into the shop today. He told us he'd been mugged last night. He brought his brother in for prayer. He'd been in a car accident three years ago and had smashed his elbow. He had titanium pins and plates holding the bones together. He showed us a huge scar and he couldn't straighten his arm. He was in a lot of pain. We got the video rolling, we prayed and he felt a lot of heat. Then his arm began to tingle and I could see it vibrating. My hands shook too but nothing else seemed to happen, even though we prayed a few times. I could feel the power of God strongly but he was still unable to straighten his arm. He told us that he's having an operation on Wednesday to remove the plates and try to straighten it so I really wanted the power of God to do it so he didn't need another op.

I could tell that there were people he needed to forgive but he wasn't interested in forgiving them. That's sad. Maybe that's why he couldn't receive the healing.

Ten Catholic ladies from Liverpool saw our sign and came in. All of them needed a miracle so I took them down to the coffee area and asked them to sit down. One said she'd had an aneurism behind her eye and that because there were no veins there any more she was completely blind and would never see again. She couldn't even see light. I placed my hand over her eye and commanded the blindness to leave and sight to come. She tested it out and could see light! We prayed again and this time she could see people moving. So we continued to speak to the blindness and told it to leave and gradually over a few minutes her sight returned. She could see what her friends were wearing, colours were bright and she was ecstatic. The doctors had told her there was nothing they could do.

One of her friends was stone deaf in her left ear. I asked how long she had been deaf for and she explained that she was so shocked when her husband suddenly died a few years ago that her ear stopped working and she has been deaf ever since. I guessed it was an evil spirit that caused the deafness, so we told it to leave and suddenly she could hear perfectly through that ear!

All the other ladies in the group were healed too; one had sciatica all down her right leg. The pain left and she was healed. Another couldn't walk properly and said her legs were weak. After prayer she was skipping around the room and felt the strength return fully. One had osteoporosis in her foot – the pain left and she felt peace. Another had very swollen ankles and they shrank before our eyes. They were all amazed.

I thought, 'revival has broken out in our shop', as all ten ladies were healed and praising Jesus. It was wonderful.

After they left, some more ladies came in. One was a Christian and wanted emotional healing and the other one said she wasn't a Christian but that Jesus had healed her eczema when she was prayed for in our shop a while ago so she decided to bring her Christian friend in for prayer! What an amazing day.

## Saturday 30 October

The 'mock up' for my book arrived today from the printer. Love it. Just needs printing now. I'm so excited. We've been working on a new online bookshop that should go live next week and we can put my book on there to sell it. I need to sell enough copies to pay back the loan for printing it and also pay for printing my next book which I've already decided I'm going to call 'The Normal Supernatural Christian Life'.

I heard that the girl's boss I prayed for over the phone recently was free from pain and able to move for that evening only, but the next day it was bad again. So apparently his Christian employee prayed for it at work. As she put her hand on his back to pray she felt something moving around under the skin and it freaked her out. I told her it could have been the metal dissolving or the bones reconstructing, or was more likely an evil spirit moving about. I know it sounds weird but we've had that happen before. Anyway, he said his back is better and he feels fine!

## Sunday 31 October

We had a great church meeting this morning with lots of people joining. It was an 'open mic' meeting which I always love. It's so good to hear testimonies and thoughts from everyone, whether they're new

Christians or have been around a while! We regularly have open mic meetings.

It's Halloween today and I decided it would be fun to knock on doors offering 'Healing or Blessing' instead of 'Trick or Treat'. Julia and Sarah joined me, and my son came with us because he wanted to see a miracle close up, which he did!

We decided to go to one of the roughest roads in Blacon. We knocked on one door and got chatting to a lady who told us she wanted to get saved, so she did. She knows Terry Fingers and told us she was amazed when he told her about his miracle with the glass coming out of his fingers and foot. At another house we met a young guy who also got saved. We prayed for quite a few people on their doorsteps.

As we were walking past the shops next to our café we saw Michael and some of his friends. He was the first person to be healed when we opened our café last year and was the one who wielded the sword at our 'School of the Spirit' meeting, the night he got saved. We went up and said hello. He told us he'd sprained his ankle playing football and also had a trapped nerve in his back. We prayed and he was healed of both problems instantly. He asked if we could prophesy to him. Julia started to get words of knowledge about the fact that he couldn't sleep and then prayed for him to sleep well. He was freaked out.

Just then, a police car pulled up. Michael is well known to the police, so they probably wondered what was going on. I approached the police car and the policeman wound down his window. Completely forgetting that I was in fancy dress I said, "It's OK officer, I'm a Christian Minister and we're just prophesying and doing some miracles." He looked me up and down, raised his eyes heavenwards, shook his head and drove off!

One of Michael's friends, Joe, was sitting on his bicycle. Michael said to him, "Come on let's do a miracle on you", so Joe rolled up his jogging pants and showed us a bony projection under his knee. It was quite big and he said it was painful. He said, "There's no point, it'll never go", as that's what the doctors had told him. But Michael insisted he let us pray. In fact I said, "Come on Michael, you can do the miracle – you have the same Holy Spirit in you that raised Jesus from the dead", so Michael put his hand on Joe's knee and he told the lump to go in the name of Jesus. To their surprise, when Michael removed his hand the lump had completely disappeared. They were both freaked out. Joe was so shocked that he got saved there and then!

Four teenage girls were watching from a distance so we went up to them and explained what had just happened. We asked if they would like to experience the presence of Jesus to which they replied, "Yeah, go on then." So we got them all holding hands and released the Holy Spirit. They all asked Jesus to forgive them for their sins and come into their lives and then the Holy Spirit came, making them giggle and feel butterflies in their stomachs and a weird feeling in their legs! What a great night. Thank you Jesus!!

*Picture of Michael from video still*

# Chapter Eleven
## November

"I have given you authority to trample on snakes and scorpions and to overcome all the power of the enemy; nothing will harm you" Luke 10:19

*"Jesus is my habit now..."*

# *Monday 1 November*

I had a day off today, although I did a bit of work too. I love what I do; following the Holy Spirit is my lifestyle, so it's difficult to have a day without 'working'.

I popped into 'Spirit' for a coffee and to see Margaret, our Shop Manager, who's back from her holiday. A woman came in whom I recognised as a customer from our Blacon café. She'd seen the sign for free miracles on her way back home from a doctor's appointment. Her lungs were damaged and she had scar tissue resulting from undiagnosed asthma. She had problems breathing, had a bad cough and told me she couldn't walk far. The doctor said she needed an x-ray. She sat down and I suggested she breathe in the Holy Spirit. She felt her lungs tingle, her cough disappeared and she was breathing normally. She said the problems had gone.

As often happens when someone realises they are healed, she went on to explain about another condition she had and asked if Jesus would heal that too. She had a cyst on one of her ovaries which she could feel through her skin and it was painful.

I asked her to place her hand on her abdomen, placed my hand on top of hers and told the cyst to disappear in the name of Jesus. I told her to feel for the cyst. She kept prodding but discovered that she couldn't find the lump any more, plus the pain had disappeared. I took some video of her testimony. Then she told me she had arthritis in her knees and hands. They were painful and stiff – that was all healed too.

Then Rob and I went out for lunch.

## Tuesday 2 November

There were no healing miracles to report from the café today. Most of the regulars who come in have already been healed and asked Jesus to come into their lives, but it's wonderful to see how their circumstances, relationships and lifestyles are changing for the better. We have employed Sarah to work in our Blacon café as a part time staff member. The grant scheme we've been awarded for six months is a great way of employing staff and we've managed to obtain funding for six people for six months. Sarah and Shelley are helping to look after and mentor many of the customers, and the café is really becoming a safe place for many people to come, some on a daily basis. I've heard customers say that it's family for them.

Ian is volunteering every Tuesday. It's wonderful to hear him praising God in the kitchen and telling everyone how he was in prison seven times, on crack cocaine and heroin for twenty seven years but that Jesus is his habit now.

## Wednesday 3 November

We had a BBQ and bonfire with fireworks tonight in our garden. It was really cold all day and raining heavily. Sarah wrote on my face book wall, "Weather bad, what time is bonfire?" I replied, "6.30pm. Think I'll go and tell the rain to stop now." She then put, "Yes, I thought you probably would." I leaned out of the window and told it to stop raining until after we'd finished for the evening. Immediately the rain stopped and the evening warmed up.

We had a great time, lots of people came, and after we finished and everyone left it began to rain again. I was outside for the fireworks without my coat it was so mild!

## Thursday 4 November

It was the 'Link Up' church leaders' prayer breakfast this morning. We were discussing whether the Chester churches should financially support a Christian bookshop that has just opened in Chester. The organisation that opened the bookshop would like to establish a large coffee bar and bookshop on the same street that we're on. They told us they're losing a lot of money and need backing so they're asking the churches to fund it and need millions of pounds. All the churches decided unanimously against it; I think most of the churches are operating on a shoe string and since we're providing a similar thing in Chester it didn't make sense. In addition, we're also demonstrating the power of Jesus, having regular input into people's lives and seeing them come to know the Lord. We often signpost these people to local church ministries near their homes.

I counted up the number of people that I know of, who have given their lives to Jesus this year in our café and our shop. The total so far is one hundred and eleven. The number of healings I've witnessed in those places comes to over two hundred. And that doesn't include the rest of the people we're training who are reaching out to others and seeing lives changed too. I've decided it's too difficult to count them up and I don't really want to keep score. The main thing is that these people are being given an opportunity to know Jesus as their Saviour and become his disciples. One of the things I find easy is introducing people to Jesus. Providing a place such as a shop, café or church group is a great way of releasing other people to get involved in mentoring and encouraging those who have just met Jesus.

## Friday 5 November

I spoke at 'School of the Spirit' tonight on 'Baptism in the Holy Spirit'. I felt inadequate and unable to articulate well what I wanted to share. However, we had a wonderful time of worship with Rob leading; loud and heavy - just how I like it.

## Saturday 6 November

Rob and I worked in 'Spirit' shop this afternoon. A woman with arthritis and needing a walking stick said she felt wonderful, peaceful and free from pain after we prayed with her. Her deaf ear didn't improve though, at least not immediately. Her husband said he was an atheist who did hypnosis. I told him we'd prayed for an atheist who was healed of sciatica. He said he had sciatica too but wouldn't let me pray for him.

Later a woman came in wanting to buy a blackboard. The only one we had left was our sign outside the shop which states, "Free Healings, Miracles & Dream Interpretation". I told her she could buy that one so I sold it to her for £25. I thought it would have been churlish to say "no". She wasn't a Christian and wasn't really interested in what the sign said, she just wanted the blackboard. But as she was paying for it I asked her if she would like a miracle to go with her miracle sign. She did. Her hands were riddled with arthritis; they were painful and stiff to move. I took hold of her hands across the counter and released the power of Jesus. She smiled and told me all the pain had gone. She was able to move her fingers freely. She thanked me for the miracle sign and the miracle and off she went with the blackboard underneath her arm.

A guy came in from a local church. He had a lump on the back of his hand which shrank as we prayed and he was able to move it without any stiffness.

I can't wait for my books to arrive from the printers. Shouldn't be long now!

## Sunday 7 November

We had our church gathering this morning. During worship, the fingers on both my hands began to tingle and then my left ear went deaf for a couple of seconds, then my right knee began to give way. Rob spoke, and near the end of his talk I felt someone poke me sharply at the base of my spine, but no-one was there.

I mentioned it to everyone, as I thought it was a word of knowledge, but nobody responded. I'm sure at least one person there could have been healed. A guy visiting said that he had the same sensation in the meeting too.

Our North Wales gathering was tonight. We had a lovely worship time and then Adrian gave his testimony of how he had been a medium before getting saved in our café last year.

## Monday 8 November

We had a day off today. I tried not to work. We went out for lunch then I popped to the Post Office. The guy in the queue behind me had a cast on his arm. As it's my day off I decided not to offer to pray for him, but then afterwards I felt really bad, then there was someone else in the supermarket I would have normally prayed for but I chose not to. They could have been healed. I don't think I'll do that again. I feel embarrassed if I offer to pray for someone and mean if I don't. I need to talk to the Holy Spirit and find out what He thinks.

I've been asked to speak at MorningStar University and at their High school when I go in three week's time. I'm looking forward to going to MorningStar and then enjoying a much needed break with my brother, along with the rest of my family.

## Tuesday 9 November

We had a great day in the Blacon café - pretty busy too. I interviewed two people for jobs. One of them would be great but she doesn't have transport and lives in North Wales. The other one is not a Christian. He's a local teenager who lives close to the café. I explained that if he works in the café, part of his job would be to learn how to do miracles, hear God's voice and follow Jesus. He said, "Great! When can I start?"

An older couple came into the café. They were in the church meeting on Sunday and I found out that the wife has a deaf left ear, but she didn't respond to the word of knowledge I had. Anyway, I told it to open in the name of Jesus and it did. I whispered in it and she could hear me perfectly.

A workman and his mate came in. He had two broken fingers. Sarah asked if she could pray and he said she could but nothing would happen as they're broken. We prayed and he said, "I'm not joking. Honest. The pain has just left." Then he moved them and was blown away by the miracle. He said if they stay like that he'll come back and give us a kiss! It was so funny. We also prayed for a young guy who had rhino-sinusitis and asthma. He felt heat in his chest and said he'll know if he's healed when he plays footie.

## Thursday 11 November

Margaret and I went to the wholesalers today and bought some Christmas decorations to sell in the shop. Then we both went for some lunch and back to the shop where a big delivery arrived so we spent the afternoon unpacking that, pricing it up and putting it out. We had to move the older stock upstairs ready for the January sale.

While we were in the middle of unpacking the delivery, three older ladies came into the shop. One had a condition like bronchitis that wouldn't go and it sounded nasty. We prayed and she said she felt much better and had stopped coughing. She also had two crutches and told us she had metal pins in her hip and knee which she hadn't been able to bend for years. I think she said it was due to osteoporosis. After a quick prayer she was able to bend her knee fully – her friend who'd known her a long time had tears in her eyes and was so amazed she kept saying, "I've not seen her bend her knee like that" over and over. She also had bad pain in her hand and particularly down her middle finger. All that went too. One of the women said, "Maybe something brought us into the shop tonight – perhaps it was the wind!" I replied, "Yes, it was the wind of the Holy Spirit." They are so close to getting saved. We sensed her friend had a broken heart so we prayed for her.

We were in the shop unpacking the stock and dressing the windows until 10.30pm. Really tired now and ready for bed.

## Friday 12 November

It was very windy last night and two of our garden rose arches fell over. I hardly slept due to the noisy chimney above our bedroom which rattles loudly when the wind blows. I finally managed to get to sleep at almost 6am but then the alarm went. I'm usually awake long before the alarm goes but this time it woke me up.

I emailed Suzy Yaraei and arranged to meet up with her and Kamran when I get to MorningStar.

## Sunday 14 November

Julia spoke on 'lepers' today at our church gathering, then she and her husband Rob came back to our house for dinner. It's always great to see them. Still a bit tired from missing most of a night's sleep.

## Monday 15 November

We opened the Blacon café today for the first time on a Monday. Up until today it was Tuesday to Friday, but due to customer demand we're able to open on a Monday too. It helps now we've employed more staff for six months with the funding available. It was Malcolm and Phil's first day. Sarah was cooking and I just went in for a couple of hours to make sure they all knew what they were doing.

It was very busy. We were praying for Daniel who's in court today for murder when in walked Tom and Carl, two more local teens who got saved recently. They both said they really want a fresh start and to commit their lives to Jesus. We all put our hands on top of each other and prayed. Phil, our new worker who I didn't think was saved, said that he gave his life to Jesus recently while he was on his own eating his breakfast in the café!

Two workmen came in. One had fallen badly and injured his back and the top part of his leg. We prayed and the pain left. His workmate asked if Jesus could help him stop smoking so we prayed for him and got him to breathe in the Holy Spirit. His eyes closed and his head slumped forward. His workmate tried to talk to him but he couldn't answer, and then his friend said he wanted the same, so he invited the Holy Spirit to come. He said it felt great.

I went into the Post Office and noticed a woman sitting down in the pharmacy section. She had a bandage on her ankle and was carrying crutches. I asked her what had happened and she told me she'd had an operation on her Achilles tendon but it was infected and very painful. There was a huge hole in the skin that went deep and needed patching up. I began to describe some of the miracles we're seeing. Her friends gathered round and said they'd heard about our café and all the miracles happening in there. They'd even watched some of them on You Tube. I prayed for a supernatural skin graft and the woman got up and tried to walk. She told me the pain had gone and it felt OK to walk on.

Then I went into 'Spirit' shop this afternoon to help unpack another delivery that arrived. It's like Christmas every time we get new stock. I love it!

# Tuesday 16 November

I went to the food wholesalers with Sarah to buy provisions for the Blacon café and 'Spirit' shop. We dropped off the food at the café and a friend of mine was there with her neighbour who had endometriosis. We prayed and she felt heat. I asked her if she would like to know Jesus and she said she did, so my friend led her in prayer and she gave her life to Jesus. She asked God to forgive her and committed her life to Him. She told us she felt "funny in a good way".

Shop sales are going well but we've been told we have to start paying rent for the Blacon café in January and that hasn't been turning over enough money to pay rent, so I'm wondering what to do.

*Picking up my books*

I got a call from the printers to say my books are ready!!! I was so excited I instantly made a round trip of five hours to pick them up instead of ordering a delivery. I just about managed to fit 25 boxes in the car. My new book looks wonderful. I hope I sell some and I'm wondering if anyone will want to buy one. I'd like to sell enough to pay my parents back for the loan by Christmas. I can't imagine being able to do that, but you never know! Rob's done an amazing job with the design.

## Wednesday 17 November

I took my books to 'Spirit' shop and dropped a few off at the Blacon café on the way. Sarah told me that she'd prayed for a woman this morning in the café with a deformed arthritic finger. Apparently the pain went and her finger straightened as they watched.

Later at home, I was in the process of buying something on the internet when I heard a knock at the door. Two Mormons were standing on the doorstep in their suits. I said, "I'm sorry I can't be long as I'm in the middle of buying something online. I fundamentally disagree with you on some issues, but Jesus died for your sins and your pain," and, looking at one of them I continued, "He wants to heal your back through the power of His Holy Spirit." The one I was looking at was surprised I knew he had a back problem.

I told him if he let me pray, his back would be healed,

but he said he wasn't allowed to receive prayer and looked over his shoulder to see if anyone was watching. I asked his friend, Elder Paul, (as his name badge indicated) if he would mind Jesus healing his friend, Elder Colin. He shook his head so I asked Elder Colin if I could pray for him and he agreed. I placed my hand over his back and released the power of Jesus and instantly he was healed. He nearly fell backwards off the doorstep he was so shocked. He looked somewhat bemused. Then I said, "Great to meet you, got to dash" and quickly closed the door and went back inside to my computer.

## Thursday 18 November

Rob and I are staying with my Uncle and Aunt in Shropshire. It's good to see them along with my cousin who popped in to say hello. We all went to a conference today, near where they live, where one of my friends from MorningStar was speaking. We went and chatted to him and then I excused myself to go to the bathroom. As I was going in, a woman stopped me and said she recognised me from the internet. She said her husband had told her to look out for me at the conference in case I was there! I told her my book had just come out so she bought a copy and got me to sign it for her husband! My Uncle and Aunt bought a few copies and so did their friends.

Our online store has just gone live and I'm enjoying getting notifications each time someone buys my book. I can hardly believe anyone would want to buy it. I thought my friends would, but people I don't know are buying it too! There must be a lot of people like me who love to read about miracles and healings that Jesus does, and want to do it themselves.

## Friday 19 November

Back home and the musician Keith Luker has arrived to minister and stay with us for the weekend. We took him into 'Spirit' shop. There we met a guy who had arthritic pain in his ankle caused by a bone he broke a few years ago. After we prayed, he told us that all the pain left and he could feel heat. Also some demons left him.

A lady came into the shop complaining about our sign outside. She told us she was a Christian and said it was wrong to have a sign like that, particularly as it said, "Today! Free Healings & Miracles." She said we were implying that it wasn't always free. I asked her if she wanted any prayer for pain in her body but she said, "No I don't. How do you know I have pain?" and off she went.

'School of the Spirit' was great tonight with Keith Luker. We had a wonderful time of worship and then we were praying for each other. It's funny but the last three Friday night meetings, Tim Morley, Keith and I all spoke on Acts 2 and we had no idea that each of us was doing that.

## Saturday 20 November

We had a late night last night and an early start this morning. Keith has gone to Belfast and will be back again tomorrow. Rob's on the men's walk up a mountain somewhere. I spent the afternoon working on my notes for preaching tomorrow.

## Monday 22 November

I didn't really end up preaching yesterday as the worship took off and we didn't want to stop. Four times over four nights in the past week, I've had dreams where I've been praying for people. It's mainly those who don't know Jesus and most of them have been young people. Each time I pray for them in my dreams they get whacked by the Holy Spirit and slump to the ground! In the fourth dream I prayed for someone who had a bad leg and a polyp on her neck, she got healed and we both got whacked by the Holy Spirit and we ended up on the floor. The following night, Rob had a similar dream where lots of young people got whacked by the Holy Spirit and so was he.

Keith Luker led worship and spoke at our North Wales gathering last night and we had a great time. Then we had fish and chips on the way home.

We went to the Blacon café with Keith today and saw Sarah; it's been one year since her son Nathan died. She's doing so well. We saw Andrew who described how he'd left his body when I prayed for him and how he'll never forget it for the rest of his life. He said his spirit went high up in the air and he was separated from his body, but it came back again before I finished praying! And he had never before encountered Jesus, until then.

A guy called Matt said he had sciatica for the past twenty years but today it left when we prayed for him.

*Keith in Café Life*

We went into 'Spirit' shop this afternoon for a coffee. People were buying my book and asking me to sign it! I must have sold 100 copies already, without even promoting it. Thank you Jesus!

A woman came in after seeing the sign for free miracles and told us she wanted to be free from anxiety and depression. I talked to her about Jesus and she said she's been thinking of becoming a Christian, although the Jehovah's Witnesses have been round trying to convince her to become a JW. She didn't like the thought of having no Christmas, so I don't think she'll become a JW. She prayed and gave her life to Jesus after forgiving her partner. I suggested she tell the anxiety and despair to leave so she did and felt it go. She said she was feeling good and light. It just so happens that she lives round the corner from Julia so I got her phone number and told her that Julia would contact her.

Last night at the meeting, Keith was getting us to break off 'disqualification' in our lives, preaching a message from Colossians 1. I broke off words that a prominent Christian leader once spoke over me that I knew were not from God. He had told me I was demonised after I shared with him some of the things God had called me to do, mainly because he felt God would not call a woman into that kind of ministry. So last night I broke the words off together with any effect they have had on my life and I forgave him. Today I found out that the Christian leader has just died. I'm very sad that he's died. I realised now he's with the Lord he's cheering me on! It's amazing how a heavenly perspective changes things.

## Tuesday 23 November

I thought I'd have a go at shopping online for my groceries since I'm busy and I had an offer of free delivery on my first order. The delivery man came with the groceries today but could hardly move as he'd pulled a muscle in his back and the painkillers he'd taken had worn off. I prayed for him and he was surprised as the pain left immediately.

A guy in the café this morning had a bad shoulder and couldn't move his arm. After prayer he was swinging it around with no problem and said all the pain had gone. We also prayed for his heart.

One of my spiritual sons, Dan, is in the middle of a murder trial, so we've been praying for him. We've been to visit him a few times in prison, and we're praying that justice would be done and the right people would be found guilty and the innocent ones would be set free. I chatted to his dad in the café today. The trial has made front page news in the local paper for the past two weeks but it reads as though Dan's guilty when in actual fact he is supposed to be innocent until proven guilty. The photo of him they're showing makes him look terrible.

Our new staff members seem to be doing well.

### Wednesday 24 November

I visited some people today and then for family activity night we watched Iron Man 2 and had a curry from the supermarket.

# Thursday 25 November

We had late night opening in 'Spirit' shop this evening and I did a book signing. It went well and the shop was packed out with lots of people who wanted to buy my new book! I sold well over one hundred books and we also sold some furniture. It was great to see so many friends and well-wishers.

*Book signing in Spirit shop*

A guy rang the shop and said that he'd bought my new book a couple of days ago and he was so stirred up in his faith that he prayed for a guy with sciatica where he works in a homeless centre and he was instantly healed. He also did some more miracles. Come on! I'm so excited. Now that's what I'm talking about!!

At the book signing we prayed for a woman who has ME and arthritis. She used a crutch as her knee was so bad. She said the pain left her knee and she walked out without a crutch.

A guy from a local church came into the book launch and told me that his thumb wouldn't move properly. He'd been told by the doctor that there was some grit in the tendon. We prayed and told it to come out when suddenly a lump appeared on his thumb and he was in pain. The lump hadn't been there before and he hadn't had any pain. It was very strange. He had a bit more movement and reckoned the lump was the grit coming out. Maybe we should have told the grit to disappear rather than come out!

Sarah is doing well in the Blacon café. She led someone to the Lord today – it was a friend of Ian's who came in for a miracle. Apparently, a child with a chest infection was also healed. Thank you Jesus! Julia arranged to see the lady who got saved in 'Spirit' shop on Monday.

It was the last 'School of the Spirit' meeting this year. We've been going for four years today, every Friday. It was snowing but still quite a good turnout. It involves a lot of work for Rob and me – setting up the PA, putting the chairs out, worship, preaching, ministry and putting it all away again. But it's definitely worth it. We're training and inspiring a lot of people who are going out and doing the stuff.

# Saturday 27th November

This week I received a letter from a solicitor declaring I will receive a CCJ (County Court Judgment) for an internet bill that I definitely do not owe (to a company called Demon!). Rob received a similar letter from Customs & Excise saying that he owed them money but he doesn't. Our son had a letter stating he was being given detention for something he has no knowledge of and our daughter received a letter saying she owes money for a train journey. Also the supermarket took £300 out of our bank account for no apparent reason!! I wonder what's going on!? We know that one of the enemy's tactics is to accuse us of acting illegally when we know we have done nothing wrong (like in the book of Nehemiah). I think we must be about to receive a huge break through... (By the way, all these things were sorted out in the end, thank you Lord).

I worked in 'Spirit' shop this afternoon. It was very busy. We prayed with quite a few people. I approached a young man and asked him if he wanted prayer. He told me he was gay and that God didn't like him because of that. But I told him how much Jesus loves him and how He died on the cross for him. He let me pray so I prayed a blessing and that he'd know God's love and would personally know Jesus.

Two women came in asking if I wanted to buy their home made cards to sell in the shop so I sat down with them for a chat. It turned out that one of them had a problem with her knee. She didn't know Jesus but let us pray for her and she felt something happening, although she wouldn't know if she was healed until she went for a long walk. We prophesied to them and they both began to get emotional. They told us that they "sort of know Jesus" and had been thinking of going to church but didn't want anything too traditional. I took their details and offered to put them in touch with some Christians who live near them.

We prayed for a few other people too for healing and other stuff and witnessed a number of miracles as usual!

## Sunday 28 November

We all felt the presence of Jesus really strongly in our church gathering this morning. I love the presence of Jesus. It was an open mic meeting. It's so good hearing from a mixture of people.

I was packing today as I leave for America on Monday for a month! But not much space for clothes as I'm trying to fit plenty of books in my suitcase to take to MorningStar.

## Monday 29 November

I flew to America today on my own. I came to Charlotte, NC via Orlando. It's so good to be at MorningStar again. Love it here. I'm here for the MorningStar Church Pastors Retreat. It seemed quiet this evening. I had a cup of tea and managed to find something to eat. The 'Oak Initiative' had a social evening with a buffet dinner and I walked in just as they were finishing so I managed to get some good food. (The Oak Initiative is a grassroots movement to unite, mobilize, equip and activate Christians to be the salt and light they are called to be by engaging in the great issues of our time from a sound biblical worldview).

## Tuesday 30 November

I awoke at 2am and couldn't get back to sleep, which means I was awake yesterday for 21 hours and only got 3 or 4 hours sleep last night. I went down at 8am and met some of the gang (the MorningStar pastors). It really is like being with family when we get together. We were just in the middle of breakfast when Tom Hardiman suggested we all go down to MorningStar University at the other end of the building and prophesy to the students, so we did that for the rest of the morning.

After lunch I spoke at MorningStar's K-12 School, 'Comenius School for Creative Leadership'. Our children, Romany and Phoenix, went to this school when we lived here for a year. They loved it. Some of the kids there remembered our children and asked after them. I encouraged the teenagers to pray for each other and to ask the Holy Spirit for words of knowledge. There were some healings too – broken arms, wrists and a girl whose broken arm four years ago hadn't set. It bent the wrong way but when we prayed it began to move and started to bend back to the correct position. She had strength in it again too.

I saw Rick Joyner at dinner and gave him a copy of my new book and thanked him for writing an endorsement for it.

# Chapter Twelve

## December

"Commit to the Lord whatever you do and He will establish your plans." Proverbs 16:3

Shelley and Sarah in Café Life

## *Wednesday 1 December*

This morning I was one of the members on the panel discussion at MorningStar University. The theme was the 'Seven Mountain Mandate' that Lance Wallnau has been teaching, and we were invited to share some of the work we are involved with that fits this Biblical Kingdom model.

We went on an outing to the 'Billy Graham Library' this afternoon, which was only about a twenty minute drive from MorningStar. It was so inspiring to see the extraordinary life of Billy Graham unfold before us with photographs, tributes and memorabilia. I remember going to Liverpool Football Stadium in the 1970s to hear this wonderful man preach about Jesus and invite people to come forward and give their lives to Him.

## *Thursday 2 December*

I'm enjoying socialising with people from other MorningStar Fellowship Churches. As part of our retreat we all had a back massage today in one of the rooms here - very relaxing. The woman who massaged my back asked me what I did. She used to come to Heritage, (the property that MorningStar now owns) when it was built by Jim Bakker. She said she is no longer following Jesus, so I encouraged her by sharing some of the miracle stories from our café and shop in Chester. She seemed captivated and wanted to know more, so I gave her a copy of my book.

Rick Joyner mentioned that he'd like to come to Chester when we hold our Prophetic Roundtable again next year. Wow! I suggested that if he wanted to come, we would like to organise a proper conference, not just a roundtable, and invite him to speak. It looks like it will happen. We've just got to find a venue now!

We've been visiting Dan, one of our young guys from the café who is in prison on remand for murder. The court case has been going for the past few weeks. As a church, we've been praying that justice would be done. I just received a text to say he has been found 'not guilty'. I cried. I'm so pleased. He is now out of prison and able to begin a new life.

I love reading Face Book updates from Sarah Roberts who's back home in Blacon working in the café with Shelley and the others. Here's a status she just posted: "A guy's leg had been really messed up for three months and he came into the café today. He was struggling a lot with it. We prayed and he felt a deep heat all over and the pain went. He'd been limping for three months but not anymore! He told a friend on the phone and then asked Jesus into his life. I also prayed for a workman's back that went hot and he legged out of the café, a bit freaked... think he had a shock!"

## Friday 3 December

It's our 22nd wedding anniversary today! Unfortunately Rob is in the UK and I'm in America and I'm missing him a lot. We don't like being apart but I'm seeing him again soon. He sent me a huge bouquet of flowers in a vase.

*A nice surprise*

The University students prophesied to us today. I videoed all the words I received. They are so encouraging and very powerful. When I get home I'll write them up into my prophetic journal. I keep a record of all the prophetic words I receive along with the dates I was given them, providing I know they're from God. It's important to read over prophetic words, pray into them and declare them until they happen.

I met up with Suzy and Kamran Yaraei this evening. I prayed for Kamran's brother over the phone. I think he's had an eye operation and was in a lot of pain. His eyes were healed as I was praying. Suzy and Kamran took me to All Nations Church (Mahesh Chavda's place) just round the corner from MorningStar. Suzy was leading worship there this evening. We had a great time. Suzy announced to everyone that I was there and introduced me and at the end I prayed with people who needed healing and deliverance.

It turns out that Suzy and Kamran will be in the UK the same time we're going to do the conference with Rick Joyner in June. And they have nothing fixed yet for those dates, so I invited them to come, lead worship and speak. This conference is coming together very easily!

## Saturday 4 December

I said goodbye to most people and spent lunchtime with some friends at MorningStar. Then we all went out in the evening for pizza and had a great laugh telling funny stories. Good times!

## Sunday 5 December

I sat on the front row next to more friends during the Sunday service this morning at MorningStar. Molly Williams led worship which I always love. Then I went for lunch with my friends Heidi and David; just a quick visit – it's always good to see them, they're wonderful people.

All the books I brought with me have gone. I think it's amazing that people actually want them and it's a shame I couldn't fit more into my luggage as more people wanted them and were disappointed I'd run out.

This afternoon I caught a flight from Charlotte to Orlando where my brother and his family live. He picked me up from the airport. It's great to be here. The weather is sunny and warm, I get to sit by the pool every day and hot tub in the evening, I'm staying in a huge en-suite room and spending time with family. All I need now is for my husband and children to arrive and thankfully they're coming soon.

## Monday 6 December

The weather has turned cold and we're all shivering. It wasn't what I was expecting in Florida! My 7 year old niece went outside in bare feet and got cold. When she came in she was shivering so I suggested she may like some Holy Spirit fire to warm her up! She agreed, so I took her hands and released the Holy Spirit. She began to giggle as she felt heat going up her arms and over her whole body. Then her legs began to buckle and she collapsed onto the floor and didn't move for ages. Her brother said he wanted some too, so I did the same thing with him. He began to laugh and fell over. The two of them were lying in a heap on the floor enjoying themselves for quite a while. Then my sister-in-law and I noticed the dog trying to walk across the room but the presence of the Lord was so thick that the little dog couldn't move. He stood in the room as though in a trance for a while, it was so funny!

*My nephew and niece – totally whacked!*

## Tuesday 7 December

Rob and our son Phoenix arrived today! It's absolutely freezing here. It's too cold to go outside so I'm sitting in the house with a blanket around my shoulders writing my next book. Are we in Florida!? It feels like we're still in the UK, although I noticed that back home it's below freezing and deep in snow. It isn't quite that bad here, but it is frosty. I think it's unusual for Florida.

My niece and nephew returned home from school to say they were still whacked from yesterday. Their friends and teachers wondered what had happened to them! They were happy about it though, thankfully.

## Wednesday 8 December

Here's a status from Sarah's Face Book update today: "Just prayed for the pizza delivery guy. He had a sore throat. He felt something happen and his voice just returned to normal. He said he has more things that need praying for and is going to pop into the café."

## Saturday 11 December

Rob and I drove down to Ft Lauderdale. We walked on the warm sandy beach which was idyllic until I trod on a bee. It felt as though I'd trodden on glass. Rob pulled out the sting and it felt OK but later on it hurt and itched a lot. We went to the Olive Garden for a meal. I had my favourite: 'Tour of Italy' which is basically three meals in one, and I can never eat it all. Then we drove to Randy and Dawn Cutter's house in Coral Springs. His brother, sister and mother were there too. They're lovely people.

Our daughter Romany arrived at my brother's today in Florida. She flew in after the others as she had an extra week at college. She's going to stay into the New Year though.

# Sunday 12 December

We had a wonderful morning. We spoke at New Dawn Church in Coral Springs. Rob spoke on the cycle of faith, hope and love. I shared some stories and encouraged people to pray for each other. When I asked who was in pain, almost everyone responded! I can't remember all the miracles, but there was a line of people wanting to give testimonies. Some of the symptoms healed were deaf ears and a girl with an inexplicable pain in the chest. She'd had tests but they couldn't find what the cause of it was. Normally that means it's a demon. We prayed and the pain moved downwards and then it left. A lump in someone's breast shrank and a woman with a dropped bladder said she felt it move back. Whilst we were praying for healing, a woman rang her mother and we released healing over the phone. She had been suffering from tinnitus – there was a loud noise constantly in her ears. The woman passed me the phone and all I could hear was a Spanish speaking woman crying loudly saying, "Thank you! Thank you!" Jesus had healed her and the noise had completely disappeared.

This evening Rob and I spoke at the Christmas dinner fundraiser at a Country Club. Each year the guests give the proceeds to charity and this year they chose to donate the money to our café. Wow. We are overwhelmed. What an amazing weekend. Thank you Lord.

## Monday 13 December

We drove back up to my brother's house in Central Florida. It took us almost four hours. When we arrived, I bit into a chilled white chocolate Santa on a stick and unfortunately broke the veneer on my front tooth in half. So now I have a painful itchy swollen foot and a broken tooth. The weather is still very cold.

## Thursday 16 December

Here's an update I just read on Face Book from Sarah back home: "A homeless guy just gave his life to the Lord in the café. He could feel the presence of God strongly. Also a customer's Grandmother got some healing for arthritis and asked Jesus into her life. And a younger guy got some healing for a spine injury. He was jumping up and down because the pain had left."

## Saturday 18 December

We are having a lovely relaxing time and the weather is beginning to warm up again. Rob, Phoenix and I went to Universal Studios yesterday and then the Hard Rock Café for dinner. We stopped for a while to watch a live band in City Walk. It's been a good day.

I've just finished reading about William and Catherine Booth and Kathryn Kuhlman and at the end of each, both write about giving the whole of oneself to God, sacrificing and offering all for Him to use. That's the secret of achieving great things for Him. I want to do that.

This evening my brother's ex-pat neighbours came round for drinks. One woman had brought her father-in-law with her. He was deaf in his left ear and wore a hearing aid in his right ear, so it was difficult for him to join in the conversation. I offered to pray for him; he could then hear his daughter whisper in both his ears. I also prayed for his knee. He told me he had rheumatoid arthritis in it and when he walks more than a few paces it gets painful and stiff. He began to feel a tingling sensation as I prayed and at the same time he looked quite surprised. I told them all about Jesus, why He died and how much He loves them.

## *Monday 20 December*

Here's another status from Sarah's Face Book update: "A drug dealer was driving through Blacon and despite the fact that he'd eaten, he suddenly got really hungry and began to look for a café. He came in and I got chatting to him. It turned out he was dissatisfied with his life. He stayed for ages and gave his life to Jesus. He was really genuine."

## *Wednesday 22 December*

Face Book status from Sarah today: "Oh wow. I just had a 'Save the Children' collector on the doorstep. He had a knee injury. Not anymore! Said he was seriously impressed and couldn't believe it. I told him quite often God shows miracles in order that we believe in Him and he just asked Jesus into his life. Also, ear pain and deafness just healed in the café."

## Saturday 25 December

The weather has warmed up for Christmas; we sat by the pool and celebrated this morning by opening our presents and then enjoyed a wonderful Christmas meal. It always seems odd to me having Christmas in a hot climate.

*Christmas Day in Café Life*

Thinking of Sarah and the others working in the café today, back home in Blacon, Chester. They are cooking dinner for over twenty people who would otherwise be on their own for Christmas. We have an amazing team! They're not getting paid to do this... they are doing it out of love.

## Monday 27 December

Arrived back home to a snowy UK. We had such a good time in America. I feel relaxed and managed to unwind. I did lots of reading and relaxing. Thank you Lord! My brother and his wife blessed us so much with meals, car rental, lots of treats and park tickets. They are unbelievably generous.

We arrived home to find our water pipes were frozen. We got in after a long flight and wanted to put the kettle on but nothing was coming out of the taps! They may have been frozen for a while. Rob went into the garage and saw that the pipes had split, but thankfully they were still frozen. Feeling jet-lagged and having missed a night's sleep, he went and bought new pipes and plumbed them in, just in the nick of time! As soon as he'd finished, the snow began to melt and the water in the pipes defrosted. If we had arrived a few hours later, the water in the burst pipes would have melted and water poured into our house. Perfect timing. God is good! We only had to wait a few hours before we got a cup of tea and a warm shower.

The other thing we found when we came home was that the power had tripped at some point whilst we were away which meant the fridge and freezer had gone off. They had defrosted and all the food was ruined. The large chest freezer was full of food which had to be thrown away. And then I noticed that someone had stolen our bay trees in pots from outside our front door. Rob had bolted them to the ground and filled them with concrete to deter thieves but they'd still been stolen! Cheeky things.

## Thursday 30 December

I just heard that two ladies gave their lives to Jesus in 'Spirit' shop after renouncing their involvement with the occult and they're asking for someone to go and do a bit of 'house clearance' (ie get rid of evil spirits)! A couple of our church members have arranged to go round there and sort them out.

And in the Blacon café, I heard from Sarah that a woman from Wales had her ankles healed today.

## Friday 31 December

There were more miracles in the café today. The lady who had her ankles healed yesterday came back. She brought a friend who was healed of a sleep disorder. Apparently she would constantly fall asleep but as soon as she was prayed for, she felt a cloud leave her as she let out a big sigh. 'Glue ear' was healed too. There was some clicking and popping and the lady felt as though something was being pushed, then she felt something leave her neck area and came up through her ears and she could hear perfectly again! Evil spirits left and arthritis pain eased. That's my Jesus!

Wow! What another amazing year. I love following Jesus.

 *Afterword*

I contended for healing for 12 years before I saw anyone healed. I prayed, fasted, read the Bible and stepped out in faith but still no one was healed. What I have come to understand is that when you are contending for something you must not give up, no matter how difficult it is, whatever the circumstances look like or how many disappointments you face. If you keep going, one day you will have a break through. And when this happens, not only do you receive the break through personally but you also release a door for others to step through. That is what happened when I didn't give up in praying for healing and deliverance.

Not only am I now seeing most people healed and delivered when I pray for them, but other people are moving in the same things without having to contend for it like I did. That is my heart; to reach those who don't know Jesus with the love and power of the good news and to train, equip and release people to extend the Kingdom of Heaven here on earth.

**"And these signs will accompany those who believe: In my name they will drive out demons, they will place their hands on sick people, and they will get well." Mark 16:17,18**

# About the Author

Aliss Cresswell, together with her husband Rob, head up MorningStar Europe, a Christian equipping ministry based in Chester UK, where they are witnessing many miraculous healings and salvations in their shop, café, in their churches and on the streets. Aliss is an international speaker, business woman and 'miracle worker', training and equipping followers of Jesus to move in the supernatural realms and to impact the world with the love and power of the gospel.

Her books 'A Diary of Miracles' and 'The Normal Supernatural Christian Life' are inspiring many to share the good news of Jesus Christ, casting out demons and healing the sick wherever they are. Rob and Aliss have two grown children.

*For more information:*

Visit: **www.morningstareurope.org**

or email: **info@morningstareurope.org**

**www.facebook.com/alisscresswellmorningstar**

# MorningStar Europe

For more information contact:

Rob & Aliss Cresswell
MorningStar Europe
96/98 Northgate Street
Chester CH1 2HT  UK

Tel: +44 (0)1244 630054
Email: info@morningstareurope.org

**www.morningstareurope.org**
Ministry Training and Resources
MorningStar Europe eJournal
School of Ministry
Spiritual Retreat Centre
Free monthly teaching podcasts
and links to videos mentioned in this book

Additional copies of this book and
other titles are available at
**www.spiritlifestyle.org**

### The Normal Supernatural Christian Life
**by Aliss Cresswell**
This book has been written for every person who wants to see God's power demonstrated in everyday life.

### A Diary of Miracles Part I
**by Aliss Cresswell**
The amazing true story of healings and encounters in a Jesus Café.

### What Next Jesus?
**by Rob Cresswell**
Welcome to your new life in Christ. 'What Next Jesus?' is a simple guide for the new Christian to the basics of Christian living.